GREECE OBSERVED

ANDRÉ BARRET

Translated from the French by Stephen Hardman

KAYE & WARD · LONDON

OXFORD UNIVERSITY PRESS · NEW YORK

Wonders are many, and none is more wonderful than man.

SOPHOCLES, *ANTIGONE*

The prospect of a journey to Greece is the promise of happiness under a burning sun and a brilliant sky. Often this return to the origins of Western civilization is not prompted by any particular sense of awe; what the visitor seeks and enjoys is the atmosphere, the simplicity, the *joie de vivre* – qualities which, even in Antiquity, were essential elements of the birth and development of Greek culture.

Not that Greece was the beginning of everything. There were brilliant and advanced societies in Mesopotamia and Egypt more than 1,000 years before the awakening of Greece. In Crete, under the influence of these older cultures, a civilization blossomed the charm and gentility of which the Greeks were never to equal. It was in Asia Minor that civilization flourished. Today, archaeologists are able to establish that in the Neolithic period certain of the great cities of Anatolia enjoyed a harmonious and peaceable existence. Even the Persians were not as barbarous as their enemies liked to pretend; it seems that they were conscientious and just administrators, who were often less cruel in their ways than the Greeks. It must not be forgotten that the Greeks were Indo-European conquerors who had come from the north – the Achaeans around the eighteenth century BC, the Dorians around the thirteenth century – and that it took several centuries of contact with the inhabitants of the Aegean to mellow and civilize these primitive tribes. The Greek people, with its mixed ancestry, always retained the spirit of these warrior tribes. Proud, vindictive and quarrelsome, the Greeks were eventually responsible for their own misfortunes and their cities tore each other to pieces until they were subjugated, first by Philip of Macedon, then by the Romans. In vain did Aristophanes, astute like many of his compatriots, exclaim indignantly: 'While your enemies the Barbarians are approaching under arms, you are killing Hellenes and destroying their cities!'

Athens and then Sparta imposed their hegemony by force. When the Persian threat had passed, the cities of Hellas were beset by rivalry, fighting and pillage; the spirit of loyal association exemplified by some of the confederacies and amphictyonic councils of earlier times was never established among them. And when Athens lost the best part of its forces in the disastrous Peloponnesian War, honour and courage were replaced by cowardice, selfishness and defeatism. Has there ever been a scene more tragic and heart-rending than when Demosthenes, before the silent assembly of the people and with the Macedonian army approaching, called for a leader: 'A citizen! A citizen!' Furthermore, the subordinate and even servile role assigned to women, the common practice of abandoning new-born female children and the lack of elementary hygiene in the cities, were clear signs of backwardness by comparison with certain earlier societies.

Where, then, lay the strength and originality of this civilization? How can one explain the sense of admiration and gratitude which it inspires? How did this poor and numerically small nation have such a profound influence on later generations who were so different to it in faith, customs and way of life? C M Bowra seems to have pinpointed the nature of what is wrongly called 'the Greek miracle' when he wrote: 'Because they felt that they were different from other men, that they must always excel and surpass them, that a man wins his manhood through unflagging effort and unflinching risk, they broke away from the static patterns of society which elsewhere dominated their age, and inaugurated a way of life in which the prizes went to the eager and the bold, and action in all its forms was sought and honoured as the natural end of man.' The glorification of personal adventure encouraged the birth of individualism and the blossoming of man, who for the first time became truly aware of his condition, his greatness and his weaknesses, and he manifested his need for self-fulfilment and his desire to reach beyond himself. A cry like that of Antigone, *I was born for love and not for hatred!* or that of Prometheus, *I would rather be bound like a slave to this rock than see myself transformed into a faithful servant of your all-powerful God!* – called upon humanity to seek love and freedom. Without Homer, Sophocles, Euripides, Socrates, Plato and Aristotle, the history of the world would not have been the same; these poets and philosophers gave human thought its first great impetus and at the same time represent its highest achievements. A belief in the special worth of man, a preference for intelligence, courage, moderation and justice, a sense of the sacred, a poetic vision of the world and of the forces governing it, all endowed these writers with a power and savour never to be surpassed. Shunning the detail of subjective analysis, they strove to express the essential. Socrates and Plato represented good as a goal which man could approach only by effort and perseverance. When Sophocles makes Oedipus, the victim of a cruelly unjust destiny, say: 'The ordeals and the long days that I have experienced teach me not to be demanding, my pride does the rest', he expresses the courage and nobility that animated the Hellenism of the Classical period. In creating gods after their own image, the Greeks sought not perfection, but the sublimation of the qualities dear to them: an eternal beauty, a will, a vigour and a dexterity without flaws.

It is in Greece that the distinctive characteristics of our Western culture originate: science, philosophy, art, literature, political principles and judicial conceptions, all derive from Greece. Via Rome, Byzantium and Christian tradition, illuminating the Arab world at its height and then becoming the focal point of the Renaissance, the heritage of Greece has made modern man what he is, whether he likes it or not. And even if the Classical values now appear debatable, this is merely a passing phase which is no doubt necessary in order that those values may rediscover a meaning and a vitality. The thirst for understanding and for action, the quest for moderation, justice and liberty, are now a fundamental need of man; without them, life would lose its pleasure and dignity.

Athens was led to democracy by its faith in man and this institution was to prove a powerful aid to his development. Extending power to all citizens and transposing the honour of the heroic age to the level of the city-state were essentially aristocratic ideas, the principal architects of which were Clisthenes and Pericles, both related to the great family of the Alcmaeonidae. One may have reservations about a political regime in which only 'citizens' actively participated and which excluded foreigners, aliens and slaves (that is to say, some forty thousand of the four hundred thousand inhabitants of the city). But civilizations do not perform miracles; they struggle to make improvements. In the economic and social context of the time, Athens could not possibly have abolished slavery, but at least it gave slavery a more humane aspect than the other cities and it never witnessed the servile herds that populated Persia and Egypt. Athenian democracy, even if it reflected certain societies of much earlier times, was nevertheless an extraordinary episode in the history of the world. All offices and positions of responsibility, except for the selection of the military chiefs (the *strategoi*), were drawn by lot among the citizens themselves; in this way the city demonstrated its absolute confidence in and esteem for its citizens, establishing true equality and justice among them. Yet the Greeks had realized that freedom could not be lawless; for a time, one of the most remarkable achievements of their civilization was the combination of this generous conception of the rights of the individual with a keen sense of the individual's duties towards the community.

Heidegger has said that the mind of man builds palaces

but inhabits a cottage. The Greeks wished to live in the palace of their minds. They had the temerity – unlike the Marxists twenty-five centuries later – to put into practice a generous ideology which would be vulnerable to the weaknesses of men. Their institutions demanded virtue; wars, economic and social crises, the inequality of wealth which they produced and the ruin of the small landowner (the symbol of moderation and wisdom) were to destroy the harmony of their society; democracy, a victim of envy, corruption and selfishness, became demagogy. Greece thus bore witness to the duality of the human condition: its glorious aspect with the need for an ideal and a thirst for the absolute, and its darker aspect with the mediocrity of its daily appetites. She offered the world the wondrous potion of liberty and at the same time revealed its dangers, for when the potion became poisoned, Greece herself was poisoned. The dialogue of the deaf between Creon, representing order, and Antigone, representing liberty, has never ceased to resound: the universe is still seeking a harmony that will balance these profound and contradictory needs.

If Greek poetry, sculpture and architecture are always admirable and sometimes sublime, it is perhaps because in artistic creation it is easier to find a balance between the needs of self-restraint and discipline on the one hand, and those of instinct and imagination on the other. Men of talent and genius are the product of their times but, precisely because they are men of talent and genius, they are not totally *dependent* on their times. With the exception of the Italian Renaissance and of French Classicism, Western art has never rediscovered this supreme harmony between order and freedom. But, as can be seen in Homer and Aristophanes and in painted pottery, the Greeks also possessed a gift for fantasy, an irony and a zest for life which are the privileges of youthful humanity. The concern with the essential, the refusal to linger over individual emotions, gave Greek art its nobility and universality. Greece still has her message to offer: in our disillusioned age, when anarchy is striving to become a form of expression, she demonstrates that order and self-restraint stimulate artistic creation, giving it strength, brilliance and depth; she reminds us also that beauty is joy, the mysterious expression of all that is most noble and sensitive in man. No people ever lived more closely with beauty and at the same time showed a greater respect for it. Sensing that this was a supreme value, the Greeks equated it with virtue: they identified *kallos* and *agathos,* the 'beautiful' and the 'good'.

The great Roman architect Vitruvius observed that the Doric, Ionic and Corinthian styles ranged from gravity to delicacy. To look at a Greek column gives joy to the simplest mind as well as to the most sophisticated – a miraculous equation combining nobility, power and elegance to produce harmony. As artifice and vanity flourish in the modern world, one can only hope that humanity will rediscover in some new form this sense of balance and natural taste for beauty.

The Greece of today has preserved its strong and vivid colours; one finds in this country a relish for life and a warmth of heart which, in spite the vicissitudes of its history, never seem to have deserted it: a dignity, a simplicity and that heroic courage of which it gave proof yet again during the Second World War. Any moderately discerning visitor can experience the feeling evoked by Henry Miller on his discovery of Greece, even if not with quite the same keen intensity as this great lyrical writer: 'For the first time in my life, too, I had met men who were like men ought to be – that is to say, open, frank, natural, spontaneous, warm-hearted . . . men who are so full, so rich . . . They ask nothing of you except that you participate in their superabundant joy of living.' In Greece it is the simplest people who are the most appealing, as if in their dignity and solitude they have preserved the art of living, the spirit of equality that inspired the Homeric age when kings were labourers and princesses washerwomen. These folk who have remained susceptible to the responses of the heart are often reserved, but they open up like flowers: the warmth of the '*yasou!*' exchanged when clinking two glasses of *retsina* is not just a convention but a genuine wish of happiness; the handful of figs or the bunch of grapes offered by a peasant-woman at the roadside is a modest but dignified gift of human friendship.

Nowadays Greece is undergoing the rapid and brutal advent of progress; money, self-interest and bad taste are establishing their dominance here as in other countries. Amid all this false glitter, how can one hope to resist the temptations of profit and comfort and to safeguard this ancient balance of wisdom and dignity? Yet it is a fragile but comforting feature of this country that one can still find here, far from the hordes of invaders, the natural qualities of the heart. According to his temperament, the sensitive visitor will discover in Greece either the vestiges of a paradise that has been irretrievably lost, or the sign of man's potential and a reason for hope.

A.B.

1 Athens and its environs

*O you, the brilliant, you whose brow is crowned
with violets, you whom the poets celebrate,
rampart of Greece, illustrious Athens, divine city.*

Pindar

*In days of old, when the delegates of the allied nations wanted to
    make you swallow their lies,
First of all they would call you the people crowned with violets,
And when you heard 'crowned', you would immediately start
    wriggling on your buttocks.
And to tickle your vanity they talked to you of the brilliant civilization
    of Athens
And they obtained everything they wanted with that word 'brilliant' –
    brilliant like a sardine!*

Aristophanes

Nowadays the visitor usually has his first view of Greece from an aeroplane, and this is in fact an ideal introduction to the country, for perhaps no other people has been so closely bound up with its geographical environment. The eye quickly grasps the essentials: bare, grey mountains cover four-fifths of the land, dividing and isolating valleys and small plains. This territorial fragmentation was represented politically by the creation of a number of independent city-states which, after enriching Greek civilization with their originality, were then to bring about its ruin by their selfish individualism. The irregular jig-saw pattern of sea and land is another significant feature, for no country has seen its maritime vocation so clearly marked out. From the multitude of different races that occupied this poor and rugged extremity of Europe there was to emerge a vigorous, agile and enterprising type of man.

As you arrive above Athens you will see the largest plain of Attica, open towards the sea, partially enclosed by mountains and of very modest dimensions; indeed, the plain is almost entirely occupied by the city and its suburbs with their straight avenues. Then the eye discovers the Parthenon, a dazzling splash of white radiating over the city from its isolated, steep-sided rock – the Acropolis, the most beautiful and moving symbol of the most glorious of civilizations.

To the simplistic mind of man, the Parthenon is Athens and Athens is Greece. Did not Thucydides, in his epitaph

for Euripides, call the city of Pericles 'the Hellas of Hellas'? And yet one must bear in mind that the Greece of today extends over less than half of the territories occupied by the Greeks of Antiquity – the cities of Asia Minor where they settled in the second millennium BC, Sicily, southern Italy where they arrived in the middle of the eighth century BC, Cyprus and Cyrenaica, not to mention the numerous cities which they founded round the Mediterranean basin. Nor should it be forgotten that for a long time Athens was only one city-state among others and of modest importance. In the sixth century BC it was the island of Samos that could claim to be the true home of the sciences and the arts; in Asia Minor the centre of Hellenism was Miletus, whose colonial empire stretched from the Black Sea to southern Italy; even on the mainland itself, Sparta was militarily more powerful than Athens, Corinth more enterprising and beautiful, while the port of the little island of Aegina surpassed that of Phalerum in wealth and activity.

Athens owed its rise to power to the Persian wars and

its triumph at Salamis (480 BC); thereafter, a fleet of more than two hundred triremes, built within a few years under the impetus of the energetic Themistocles, was to guarantee its supremacy and prosperity. At the end of the sixth century, the Persians had pillaged and subjugated the Greek cities of Asia Minor and the nearest islands, Samos, Chios and Lesbos; at this time these rich lands of Ionia were the home of the artistic taste and the spirit of inquiry that characterized Hellas. Gathering these states together in the confederacy of Delos (477), Athens took up the torch, seizing a part of their material wealth in the form of a tribute exacted for their protection, after having assimilated their artistic and cultural attainments. But the Athenian adventure was not basely solely on borrowings. The democratic regime which Athens was to impose, in opposition to the oligarchic governments by which it was surrounded, was the achievement of its citizens and of their love of liberty, their independence, their energy and the need for personal fulfilment which was a fundamental value of the Greek ethic. The destiny of Athens was also linked with a succession of politicians of outstanding quality: Dracon, Solon, Clisthenes, Themistocles, Cimon and Pericles.

Even when embellished with legend, the origins of any great city are always modest; the city begins as a small village, which then becomes a township. According to tradition, Cecrops, the first king of Athens, came from Egypt. Theseus, the legendary hero whose renown and exploits matched the pride of the Athenians, was supposed to have liberated Athens from Cretan suzerainty. The episode of the Minotaur, the Labyrinth and Ariadne's ball of thread is well known. Theseus, the son of Zeus or of Aegeus according to the legends, and in fact probably an Achaean conqueror, brought unity to Attica, which henceforth was centred on the Acropolis and dedicated solely to the cult of Athena.

Hereditary royalty disappeared around the ninth century BC and power passed into the hands of a few great families, the Eupatridae. The government comprised the Areopagus and the *archons,* who at first numbered three and later nine. In the seventh century one of the *archons,* Dracon, gave the city its first written laws, affirming the authority of the State in matters of justice. At the beginning of the sixth century, Solon endowed Athens with its first Constitution. Henceforward, social classes were determined not by birth but by wealth: the richest persons were awarded the highest magistracies, but also the heaviest responsibilities. Pisistratus and his sons proved effective and moderate 'tyrants'; in the struggle for the ownership of land they protected the weakest and also encouraged commerce and industry. It was Clisthenes who, during a period of ten years at the end of the sixth and the beginning of the fifth centuries, really gave a structure to Athenian democracy. He divided Attica into one hundred communes (*demoi*) and increased the number of ancient tribes to ten. The senate (*boulé*) was composed of 500 members (fifty from each tribe). By its concrete nature, this new political division disregarded individual interests and passions, establishing unity among all Athenians – landowners, peasants, tradesmen and sailors. The assembly of the people (*ecclesia*), which enjoyed sovereignty in its deliberations, sat at least once during each *prytany* (a period of thirty-five to thirty-nine days); a quorum of 6,000 votes (out of the 35,000 to 40,000 citizens inhabiting Athens in the fifth century) was necessary for the most serious decisions. From the time of Solon, the citizens also played a most important part in the judicial system, for 6,000 jurors (*heliastes*) were drawn by lot every year.

The rise of Athens to the front rank of Greek cities owed much to Themistocles, the man who took the initiative, and to Aristides; the former was a *strategos*, the latter an *archon*. When danger threatened, these men were able to establish the alliance with Sparta and stir up resistance. After the victories over the Persians, it was they who, by organizing the confederacy of Delos, enabled the influence of Athens to spread over the whole of the Aegean.

When Pericles came to power, which he exercised only as a *strategos* (a military chief re-elected every year), the strength of Athens reached its peak. The city was bursting with vitality and ambition and under his government was to achieve glory in the works of Aeschylus, Sophocles, Euripides and Phidias. If the intellectual and artistic radiance of this golden age ceased only with the triumph of Christianity, on the political plane 'the century of Pericles' in fact lasted less than forty years, from 470 to 429 BC. According to Thucydides, this great man loved 'Fascist' slogans: 'We have forced every sea and every land to open up before our daring.' The extraordinary dynamism of Athens placed it firmly in the foreground of Hellas, a position which it maintained from the victory of Salamis (480) until the beginning of the ill-fated expedition to Sicily (415–13). But, although Athens conquered several Greek cities – Aegina, Samos, Miletus – and subjugated the states that had entered into a free association in the confederacy of Delos, it could never truly lay claim to a hegemony over the whole of Greece, which only regained the unity lost at the time of the Mycenaean Empire (thirteenth century) with the conquest of Philip II of Macedon (fourth century). The chief accusation that could be brought against Pericles is that he adopted a Pan-Hellenic policy, nurturing ambitions which exceeded the real strength of Athens and which thus involved it in continual warfare. In 431 BC he declared war on Sparta. This was to become the Peloponnesian War, a disastrous conflict lasting twenty-five years in the course of which Athens was to squander its strength.

It seems probable that, after the victories over the Persians, had it not been for the appetite for power, conquest and pillage manifested by the Athenian democracy, Greece might have found a happier destiny within the framework of a confederacy respectful of the liberties of each city. Unfortunately, the Athenians were far from cherishing the noble sentiments attributed to them by Herodotus when they resisted the king of Macedonia, refusing to desert the Greek cause in the struggle against the Persians: 'What unites the Greeks – the same blood, the same language, common sanctuaries and sacrifices, similar manners and customs – the Athenians ought not to betray.' The direct democracy practised by Athens was worth no more than its citizens: self-interest, ambition and social instability had rapidly taken the place of the virtues of the heroic age. Yet certain minds saw clearly. Aristophanes gave vent to his indignation: 'While your enemies the Barbarians are there in arms, you are killing Hellenes and destroying their cities.' Plato pronounced a harsh judgement when he accused Themistocles, Cimon and Pericles of having 'crammed the city with harbours, arsenals, walls, tribes and other absurdities' instead of following the path of virtue and moderation. The victory of Philip II at Chaeronea (340 BC) marked the end of free Greece; but, even as early as 404, when the Peloponnesian War had terminated with the capture of Athens by Sparta, something irreplaceable had died – an equilibrium between tradition and novelty from which Athens had drawn its austerity, its enthusiasm, its relish for life and its need of knowledge and beauty. Henceforth, Athens had a guilty conscience.

In the cities of Archaic Greece the temples, the palaces of the kings and the fortresses that would protect the population in the event of danger were built on a stretch of high ground which was partly natural and partly man-made: this sacred place was called the 'acropolis'. From the platform of the Acropolis of Athens the view embraces the whole city, which today numbers over one million inhabitants. White and fairly uniform in layout, the city is divided by straight streets; enclosed by the grey mass of the bare mountains – Ageleus, Pentelicus and Hymettus – it follows the incline of the plain, which slopes down to the sea, suddenly appears to rise as if to assault Mount Lycabettus, a conical rock situated almost in the centre of the plain, then skirts the Hill of the Nymphs and the Hill of the Muses to the south and finally reaches Piraeus, geometrically laid out with the harbour in the distance sparkling with hundreds of boats. The horizons of Athens are the grey line of mountains to the north and, to the south, the infinity of the sea.

The sanctity of the **Acropolis** was so obvious that Athena, Christ and Mahomet have been invoked there in turn. Both church and mosque have vanished, leaving only the stone masterpiece erected by the triumphant democracy to its protecting goddess. A place of revelation and veneration hewn and carved out of stone by man, the Parthenon stands witness to an ideal balance between mind and matter.

Ernest Renan's *Prière sur l'Acropole* is often mentioned, but few people are familiar with its exalted words: 'When I saw the Acropolis, I had a revelation of the divine, as I had when, for the first time, I felt the Gospel live on beholding the valley of the Jordan from the heights of Casyoun. The whole world then seemed barbarous to me. The Orient shocked me by its pomp, its ostentation, its impostures. The Romans were merely crude soldiers [. . .] I found our Middle Ages without elegance or shape, stained with misplaced pride and pedantry. Charlemagne seemed to me like a coarse German stable-man; our knights seemed bumpkins who would have made Themistocles and Alcibiades smile. There existed a people of aristocrats, a whole public composed of connoisseurs, a democracy that grasped nuances of art so delicate that our men of taste are hardly able to perceive them. There existed a public which understood what makes the beauty of the Propylaea and the superiority of the sculptures of the Parthenon. This revelation of true and simple grandeur penetrated to the depths of my being.'

In 480 BC the Persians had pillaged and burned the ancient sanctuaries and so, when the Athenians returned to their city after the victory of Salamis, they owed it to themselves to erect to their goddess a temple worthy of their new-found glory. This was one of the first undertakings on which Pericles embarked when he came to power. He chose Phidias to supervise the mighty enterprise and, in spite of the hostility to which the sculptor was subjected, never lost confidence in him. At this time architecture was still reserved for the gods. The clarity of the lines and the harmony of the volumes were the very essence of the structure; sculpture, however admirable, had only a secondary function. Yet the most precious object in this temple was the giant statue of Athena carved in ivory and gold by Phidias and placed in the *naos* or sacred chamber; the statue, some twelve metres high, doubtless determined the dimensions of the edifice (69·51 × 30·86 metres).

The **Parthenon,** with its eight façade columns, is of a squarer plan than was customary for a Doric temple. Attention has been frequently drawn to the refinements of the two architects, Ictinus and Callicrates: the swelling of the corner columns, the slight inward incline of the columns, the curvature of the foundation repeated on the architrave.

These refinements were designed to correct certain optical effects, to give the lines their full purity and the volumes their true value, although they were not totally new features in architecture. The Parthenon is facing Athens; as the visitor comes on to the Acropolis, he therefore sees it from behind. In ancient times it was at first hidden from sight by balustrades and buildings; one had to make one's way through numerous stelae and votive statues to obtain a view of the temple. What activity and enthusiasm must have filled the site as Phidias and his pupils went about their work! Little of the original statuary now remains, but there is enough to reveal these sculptures as one of the finest achievements of architecture. On the east pediment (that is, on the entrance façade of the temple) was represented the birth of Athena emerging fully armed from the head of Zeus; on the west pediment, the rivalry of Athena and Poseidon for the sovereignty of Attica. Ninety-two metopes decorated the exterior entablature, but most of them are now ruined or have disappeared (the enterprising Lord Elgin removed fifteen and took them back to London with a great many other sculptures). These metopes – the stone pictures of Antiquity – showed the battle of the Greeks against the forces of darkness and barbarism (centaurs, giants, Amazons and Trojans), thus illustrating the ideas of Anaxagoras, a philosopher and friend of Pericles, who believed that the world had been chaos before intelligence had triumphed – 'intelligence' (*nous*) being the strength and wisdom of the Greeks.

The Parthenon's masterpiece of sculpture, however, was the Ionic frieze (one hundred and sixty metres long) which ran under the peristyle and across the entire length of the temple, depicting the procession of the Greater Panathenaea. Of the many festivals held in Athens, the two most important were the Dionysia and the Panathenaea, the latter being celebrated every four years with exceptional brilliance. Priests did not play an influential role in the life of Greece, except in their capacity as soothsayers. There was no dogma and little in the way of liturgy; the worship of the gods belonged to all. The procession moved through the city in a clearly defined order: the youths (*epheboi*) on horseback, the girls carrying the embroidered *peplos* (the sacred robe made for the goddess), then the musicians, victorious athletes, women bearing offerings, the sacrificing priests escorting the oxen and sheep that were put to death by hundreds and whose flesh, once a modest portion had been offered to the goddess, was distributed to the rejoicing population.

The fact that the eye can only guess the various elements of the frieze, which still adorns the Parthenon, underlines the symbolic value of the temple's sculpture; perfectly executed, even in its hidden parts, it was above all an offering of veneration and beauty to the goddess who symbolized the city.

The **Propylaea,** the monumental entrance porch leading to the terrace of the Acropolis, were not begun until the Parthenon had been completed, in 437 BC, so as not to interfere with the building work. Under the supervision of the architect Mnesicles, the construction of the Propylaea lasted five years, but was never finished. This monument, built on several levels and with four entrance porticos, is of noble proportions. Its columns are, perhaps, the finest in Greece; as the sun sinks, they retain their luminous whiteness for a long time, while those of the Parthenon, also carved from Pentelic marble, are tinged with pink, red and then brown until they are engulfed in the blue and grey of the night.

The graceful, asymmetrical **Erechtheion** stands on the most sacred part of the Acropolis, where the first Mycenaean temple was erected. It served a variety of purposes: it once contained the tombs of the first Athenian kings and heroes: Cecrops, Erechtheus, Boutes and Pandros. It was here that Athena and Poseidon were supposed to have contended for possession of Attica: the goddess offered the olive-tree which had grown near the temple and Poseidon, with a blow of his trident, split a rock from which salt water spurted (hence the legendary origin of the cavity under the north portico, also attributed to a thunder-

bolt of Zeus). It appears that the cults observed in this highly sacred place were devoted not only to the gods, but also to the heroes of the city; in the east chamber, dedicated to Athena, was the *xoanon*, an ancient statue of olive-wood, to which the *peplos* embroidered by the maidens was carried every year during the Panathenaea.

The Erechtheion, despite its architectural imbalance (it is built on several levels), has the grace charac-teristic of the Ionic order: the coffered ceiling of the main portico, originally painted blue and decorated with bronze stars, and the delicately carved frame of the doorway are both typical of this refined art; but the eye is attracted chiefly by the Porch of the Maidens (the *korai* or maidens came to be known, incorrectly, as caryatids), which has six delightful figures of girls radiant with health and grace. The Erechtheion was built some thirty

years after the Parthenon to replace the old sanctuary. It is astonishing that such a short period separates two styles of architecture so different in spirit, one noble and vigorous, the other elegant and refined. Yet there is no break of continuity, nor even a transitional stage, between the Doric order and the Ionic order. Between 425 and 421 BC, after Athens's first victories in the Peloponnesian War, Callicrates, the architect of the

Parthenon, built the **Temple of Athena Nikē** (goddess of victory). Perched on a promontory flanking the entrance of the Propylaea, this perfectly designed temple is a model of the Ionic style. It suffered many changes of fortune: demolished in the seventeenth century to make room for a Turkish bastion, it was rebuilt and then moved to a different position. Is this, perhaps, why its elegant forms seem rather cold and its white marble remains lifeless? The Ionic frieze that adorned the temple also attracted the interest of Lord Elgin; today, partly in its original form and partly consisting of plaster reproduction, it is in a very dilapidated state. Some sculptured fragments have been found from the balustrade that ran round the terrace on which the temple stands; they represent Victories preparing a ritual sacrifice for Athena Nikē. The Acropolis Museum contains the most famous of these figures, shown fastening her sandal.

The **Acropolis Museum** houses a collection of statues and fragments of sculpture that once decorated the temples built on the sacred terrace. The exhibits are few in number but all of the greatest interest, completing the architectural study of the edifices – tufa fragments of Archaic pediments of the seventh and sixth centuries, representing lions, griffins, serpents and other monster-creatures from Asia which figured in early Greek religion. This is a robust animal art of great style.

Workmanship of a power and freedom equalled only at Olympia appears in the remnants of a sculptured group belonging to the *gigantomachia* (a battle between gods and giants), from which has survived an admirable statue of Athena that adorned the pediment of a temple of more ancient date than the Parthenon. In the fifth century BC the traditional disciplines of temple decoration were more rigorously applied; the balance of the composition of the pediment, the strict centring of the metopes and the narrowness of the frieze in relation to its length were to make the task of the Greek artists particularly difficult, though they displayed an astounding skill. These first sculptures bear traces of black, green and

red painting. The association of colour with architecture is the sign of an Eastern influence. The decorative elements of temples, and also their ceilings and walls, were painted, but the columns, unlike those of Egypt and Crete, do not seem to have been painted; at an early stage the Greeks had shown a fondness for the play of light on marble and stone.

The Acropolis Museum has another treasure to offer: the dazzling, joyous *korai*, figures of young women, discovered at the end of the nineteenth century in a ditch near the Erechtheion, where they must have been buried after the desecrations of the Persians. These marble statues of various sizes, some of them still coloured, date from the sixth century BC. Painted like Oriental women, they are mostly Ionian girls; some, however, already have the gravity characteristic of Attica. The contribution made by Eastern art in Athens was considerable; even in the time of Phidias, many of the sculptors in his workshop came from the islands and from Asia Minor. These charming young ladies with their engaging, mocking smiles are skilfully adorned with wavy hair falling over their shoulders and down their backs in long plaits; some are dressed in the Dorian *peplos*, a sober, smooth tunic, and the others wear the Ionian *chiton*, pleated and fastened at the waist, often with the *himation*, a shawl elegantly crossed over the shoulders; some of them show a bare breast. The statues now bear numbers, 679, 680, 686 and so on, but the imagination can replace these archaeological labels with names better suited to their lively eyes and coloured lips – Laïs, Erinna, Sappho, Heliodora, Cassandra, Pelagia . . . In fact, although they are all different, they are all anonymous and symbolical. In the sixth century BC art was still exclusively sacred; it was not until the end of the fifth century that the first faithful representations of a human face were to appear. Holding their robes in one hand and carrying an offerings vase or cup in the other, these radiant maidens were votive statuettes placed in a sanctuary or on a tomb.

Two very beautiful archaic statues of men also catch the eye: the *Rampin Horseman*, which owes its name to the gentleman who took its head to the Louvre Museum (the head has been replaced by a copy), and the *Moschophoros* (Calf-bearer), a figure of a sacrificing official carrying a young calf on his shoulders. This sixth-century marble has an intense power, fully justifying the judgement of the great English Hellenist C M Bowra when he writes: 'It was this sense of a connexion between the seen and the unseen, between the accidental and the essential, between the transitory and the permanent, which provided Greek art with a guiding ideal and a welcome discipline and ennobled it with an exalted detachment and a consistent, self-contained harmony.'

The Acropolis Museum also contains two admirable

series of sculptured slabs. A dozen of these come from the frieze of the Greater Panathenaea on the Parthenon: horsemen, girls carrying offerings vases (*hydria*), lyrists, and rams and heifers escorted by the men responsible for sacrificing them. This is the very peak of Classical art. The other series comprises twenty or so fragments from the balustrade of the Temple of Athena Nikē. The most famous of these Winged Victories associated with the cult of Athena has already been mentioned (the one shown fastening or unfastening her sandal). In the suppleness of the female bodies and in the harmony of the draperies, these sculptures dating from the end of the fifth century BC reveal a new sensuality and refinement. How one would love to have a more complete view of

such masterpieces! Yet these few fragments are deeply moving, for they are beauty pure and simple, enabling the imagination to re-create the rhythmic unity of these mighty compositions. Although they are only Lord Elgin's leavings, the proximity of the temples and of the sun of Attica makes them much more affecting than the admirable pieces from the east pediment of the Parthenon, the selection of the best-preserved metopes and other frieze fragments that were taken into exile to the British Museum.

After experiencing the thrill of the sublime on the Acropolis, the visitor should go down to stroll about the surroundings of the sanctuary, which prompt reflections of a different kind, recalling the daily life and political

activity of ancient Athens. On the south side of the Acropolis is the Theatre of Dionysus, largely refashioned in the Roman period and which witnessed the birth of the ancient drama. During the four days of the Greater Dionysia (the theatre was closely associated with the god Dionysus, whose cult assumed both an orgiastic and a transcendental character), the people would arrive in the morning and leave in the evening, after watching a succession of four and sometimes five tragedies or comedies by authors such as Aeschylus, Sophocles, Euripides and Aristophanes. Near the theatre stood a temple of Asclepius, the healer-god of Epidaurus whose cult was introduced in Athens towards the end of the fifth century BC, and a portico presented to the Athenians

by Attalus, king of Pergamum; at the end of the portico lies the Odeon of Herod Atticus (second century AD), the famous patron of the arts and rhetorician who presented this Roman edifice to his fellow-citizens so that they could hear music and choruses there. The absence of specific references to music often obscures the vital part which this art played in Greek life: a fundamental discipline of education, it was for the Greeks more than an art – it was a necessity. The music of the cithara, the double flute and the tambourine accompanied the important occasions of Greek life: worship, combat, banquets and the theatre; but nothing is known of the rhythms and tonalities of a musical form that was primarily vocal.

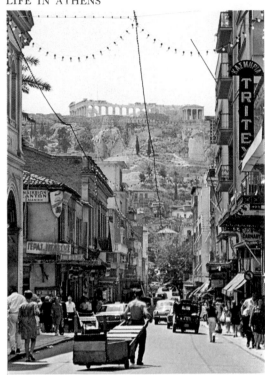

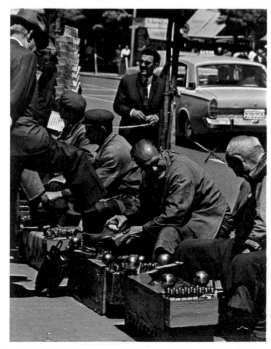

Near the Sacred Way leading to the Propylaea rise two rocky heights which, though modest in size, are famous for the role they played in the political life of the city: the **Areopagus** and the **Pnyx.** The Areopagus gave its name to a council that was originally an all-powerful tribunal. The Areopagus prided itself on having judged Ares, the god of war (hence its name), and Orestes who, pursued by the Erinyes or Eumenides (the fearsome goddesses who avenged bloodshed), had been acquitted through the eloquence of Apollo. By the time of Pericles, the Areopagus had lost all political power. Later, St Paul is believed to have addressed the Athenians here. On the Pnyx (literally, 'the place where people are crowded together') the *ecclesia* or assembly of the people gathered; of the 40,000 citizens inhabiting Athens in the Classical period, 4,000 or 5,000 would attend for ordinary matters, and double this number for more important occasions. At this very spot Themistocles, Aristides, Pericles, Alcibiades and Demosthenes had to use all their skill and eloquence to convince their fellow-citizens. In Athens, as the wise Fénelon observed, 'everything depended on the people and the people depended on the word'.

From the Areopagus you go on to the **Temple of Hephaestus** or **Hephaisteion,** which rises above the Agora. This temple, dedicated to the god of fire and of blacksmiths, was for a long time called the Theseion because its frieze (now badly ruined) commemorating the exploits of Theseus, a hero particularly dear to the hearts of Athenians. In the Doric style with Ionic elements, the Hephaisteion, though of earlier origin than the Parthenon, is in an excellent state of preservation; but it is rather lacking in imaginative power and does not possess the regal nobility of the buildings on the Acropolis. The temple adjoins the Keramikos district where the potters and smiths practised the crafts requiring the use of fire; the god Hephaestus was the protector of their activities, together with Athena Hephaesta, the goddess of the city in one of her secondary functions. The ancient surroundings of the temple have been effectively recreated by planting laurels, pomegranate-trees, myrtles and acanthi.

From the temple terrace you look on to the vast **Agora,** an indispensable part of the Greek city, for it was not only a market-square and place of public assembly, but the very symbol of social life and the seat of the various institutions of the democratic government. Power had descended from the royal Acropolis and now lay at the heart of the city. In spite of its noise and bustle, the Agora possessed a certain sacred character; water-basins were placed around it so that people could purify themselves before entering. These ruins will mean little to the non-specialist, but at the right time of day the visitor can enjoy a delightful stroll over the old paving-stones and among the fragrant rose-laurels, strawberry-trees and plants. One can see the remnants of the Tholos which accommodated the *prytanes*, the fifty senators who governed the city and who were replaced ten times every year; the Bouleuterion, where the 500 senators sat (fifty per tribe); the Temple of Apollo Patrous, supposedly the father of Ion, the ancestor of the Ionians from whom the Athenians liked to believe themselves descended; and the Portico of Zeus or Royal Portico, under which sat the king-*archon*, the supreme judge, elected annually by the drawing of lots.

In the Hellenistic period many new porticos were erected; that enclosing the east side of the Agora was presented by the king of Pergamum, Attalus II, a pupil of the Athenian philosophers; rebuilt by the American School, which began the excavation of the Agora in 1931, it now houses an excellently planned museum with an abundance of precious exhibits. Other

porticos divided the various markets (fish, poultry, wine, wood, fabrics, pottery, fruit, vegetables, cheese) where, amid the shouting, swearing and arguments, the *agoranomoi* or clerks of the market maintained order.

The shopping was usually done by the women, accompanied by their slaves; they paid with a silver coin, the drachma or obolus (one drachma = six oboli); one side of the coin bore a helmeted head of Athena, the other an owl with a crescent moon, an olive shoot and the first three letters of the word 'Athens'. The tradesmen were called *kapeloi*, a word tinged with a pejorative connotation. Most of them were 'metics' or aliens, a term which originally implied no hint of racial prejudice: literally it meant 'those who live with' and was applied to foreigners, those not born of an Athenian father and mother; they were freemen, but had no political rights in the city. The majority of the metics originated from Hellas, but they also included Phoenicians, Egyptians and even Arabs. In the fifth century BC, when they numbered about 20,000, they constituted a proportion of the

population equal to one-half of the total number of 'citizens'. Enterprising and active, many of them were tradesmen, craftsmen and soldiers; others had established themselves in leading positions in commerce as merchants, shipowners and bankers. Numerous also among physicians, artists and philosophers, the metics often played a role rather similar to that of Jewish minorities in certain countries. After they had for a long time been unreservedly welcomed in Athens, the wealth and ambition of some of their number were eventually condemned by the oligarchic governments of the fourth century BC; Plato wanted their activities to be restricted.

The visitor should stroll through the oldest part of Athens, the **Plaka** district; its picturesque outlines and the pretty roofs of Roman tiles can be seen from the view-point situated at the west extremity of the Acropolis.

If one ignores the signs of the numerous taverns which spring to life in the evenings, this part of the city has hardly changed since the Greek War of Independence (1821–1827); the little houses are delightful and there are steps everywhere. Here you will find two monuments of rare elegance: a votive column of Pentelic marble celebrating the *choregos* Lysicrates, a rich Athenian who, as was the custom, financed his tribe's chorus which had been successful at the competition held in the Dionysia; and a later structure (first century AD) called the Tower of the Winds or the Hydraulic Clock of Andronicus, hexagonal in form and decorated with graceful winged figures representing the principal winds of Attica.

On the division of the Empire of the West and the Empire of the East in AD 395, Greece naturally fell to Byzantium; despite the Slav and Bulgarian invasions and the Frankish and Venetian conquests, it was to remain under Byzantine suzerainty until the arrival of the Turks – that is to say, for more than ten centuries. Greek Byzantine

art is to be found chiefly at Salonika, Mistra and Mount Athos. But Athens contains some exquisite little churches, often in unprepossessing surroundings: the Holy Apostles (Haghii Apostoli) along the Agora, the church of Kapni-karea (Haghiou Konstantinous) and, above all, the Little Metropolis (Mikri Mitropoli, twelfth century), also called Gorgoepikoos (St Eleutherios), where the walls have a patina of old ivory and which bears a curious decoration of marble fragments of the most diverse origins: a Byzantine bestiary, antique friezes and capitals, Frankish armorial bearings and fragments of Cufic script. Visitors interested in this kind of art should also go to the Byzantine Museum, a modest but pleasant building where sculptures, icons and ornamental fabrics are exhibited; nearby the

Benaki Museum, endowed by a collector of eclectic but refined tastes, offers an astounding display of fabrics, jewellery and icons, and masterpieces of Muslim, Egyptian and Chinese art. It is also well worth taking a trip out of Athens in the late afternoon to see two little monasteries of breathtaking charm and freshness: the monastery of Kaisariani lies seven kilometres from the city, in a green vale shaded by hundred-year-old plane-trees and cypresses; the church dates from the tenth century, the bell-tower from the seventeenth; the setting is an oasis of peace and serenity – sitting by the large acanthus leaves, you can listen to the murmuring of a spring whose water supplied Athens in ancient times. On another evening taking the Sacred Way, which led from the necropolis of

the Keramikos and the Sacred Gate to Eleusis, you can go to the entrancing monastery of Daphni. The restored buildings have a rustic simplicity, but inside the church the gold and the colours of the mosaics (eleventh century) dazzle the eye; reflecting the rigorous order of Byzantine theology, they have clear, powerful lines. In the cupola the admirable and yet terrible figure of Christ Pantocrator looks down severely on his creatures.

The modern city of Athens is of little architectural interest; over the years it has suffered the political and economic instability of a poor country, but it has its own charm: vendors of lottery-tickets, nuts and sponges, shoe-blacks, photographers and newspaper-stalls give its squares the antiquated appearance of a spa around 1900.

25

Apart from the Plaka district, which unfortunately is becoming more like Montmartre every year, the city has other surprises in store for the visitor: the little Byzantine churches almost crushed between huge modern blocks and the sudden glimpses of Mount Lycabettus, Mount Hymettus, the Acropolis and the sea. The National Gardens (Zappeion), situated right in the heart of the city, have a deliciously provincial atmosphere and one can stroll pleasantly there among the fragrant plants.

A visit to the **National Museum** reveals the full splendour of Greek art and enables one to trace its evolution. Statues, bronzes and pottery bear witness to the invention, the sense of restraint and the vigour that inspired the Greeks' intense love of beauty.

Art was born on Greek soil in the fourth millennium BC with the Neolithic marble idols and terracotta pottery discovered in Thessaly, but it was in the third millennium that it really displayed its originality with the emergence of the Cycladic civilization. The contacts which these islands of the Aegean had at this period with the city-states of Mesopotamia and Anatolia, which had reached a much more advanced stage of political, social and artistic life, undoubtedly proved decisive. Troy appears to have been the centre from which the Cyclades absorbed the influence of the Anatolian Bronze Age and of the age of metalworking, linked with the pre-Hittite civilization and the working of gold, silver, copper and iron (at that time, no doubt, the most precious of metals). Trade was practised on a large scale between the coast of Asia and the islands, and waves of immigrants from Anatolia established themselves among the Aegean populations of the Neolithic period. It must also be remembered that the islands had contacts with Egypt, which had revealed great creative vigour during the first dynasties of the Old Empire. However, the art of the Cyclades was profoundly original, even if it took shape under diverse influences. The marble idols (about thirty centimetres high) carved by the craftsmen of the small towns are justly famous. Their abstract, geometric forms have a mysterious quality to which the modern eye is highly susceptible. Reduced to a form resembling that of a violin, some of them are of a stark simplicity, while others present a stylization of the body (legs close together and arms crossed) and of the head, which is in the form of a shield with only the nose and ears in relief; some figures are more elaborate, with two little breasts and the outlines of the eyes, the mouth and the sex organs. Clearly, these statuettes have a definite symbolism, but precisely what they symbolize is not known. It is thought that some of them are fertility goddesses who also played a part in the cult of the dead. The two figures of musicians in the National Museum of Athens are probably votive statuettes; in any case they prove that the lyre and the double flute, the most popular instruments of the Classical age, were already known some fifteen centuries earlier (these idols have been dated approximately in the year 2000 BC). The Cycladic civilization was to lose its originality when the islands came under the domination of Crete.

If the formation of the Cretan or Minoan civilization was influenced by Syria and Egypt, it nevertheless displayed a highly personal character by its inventiveness and refinement. Through two quite distinct periods it maintained its hegemony from 2000 to 1450–1400 BC. The Mycenaean civilization (1450–1400 to 1200 BC), which succeeded it, was the first that can truly be called Greek; it was the achievement of Indo-Europeans, the Achaeans, who must have penetrated into the Peloponnesus shortly after the year 2000 BC. For a time, before establishing themselves as the conquerors of the whole of Hellas, it seems that the Achaeans were subjected to Cretan influence and suzerainty. Recent decipherings of cryptographs have made it possible to ascertain that in Mycenae and Tiryns an archaic Greek was being spoken around 1400 BC. It is in this period that scholars have placed the origins of the Homeric epics and of a tradition that lies half-way between legend and history – the Trojan War and the sombre destiny of the family of the Atridae.

Although its architecture possessed a powerfully sober, military style, Mycenaean art seems to have remained closely dependent on that of Crete in its decorative aspects (pottery, jewellery and statuettes, though many cruder objects were also being made at this time). The influence of Minoan art in the dazzling treasures contained in the royal tombs of Mycenae seems obvious; it has been suggested that they were booty acquired by the Achaeans in their early plunderings. But the gold coverings in which the bodies of the Mycenaean kings, their wives and children were dressed suggest an original art which, in the opinion of some specialists, is the first manifestation of a monumental Indo-European plastic art. The death-masks, which have an astoundingly expressive power, were doubtless fashioned on the face of the corpse. The two famous goblets, one representing

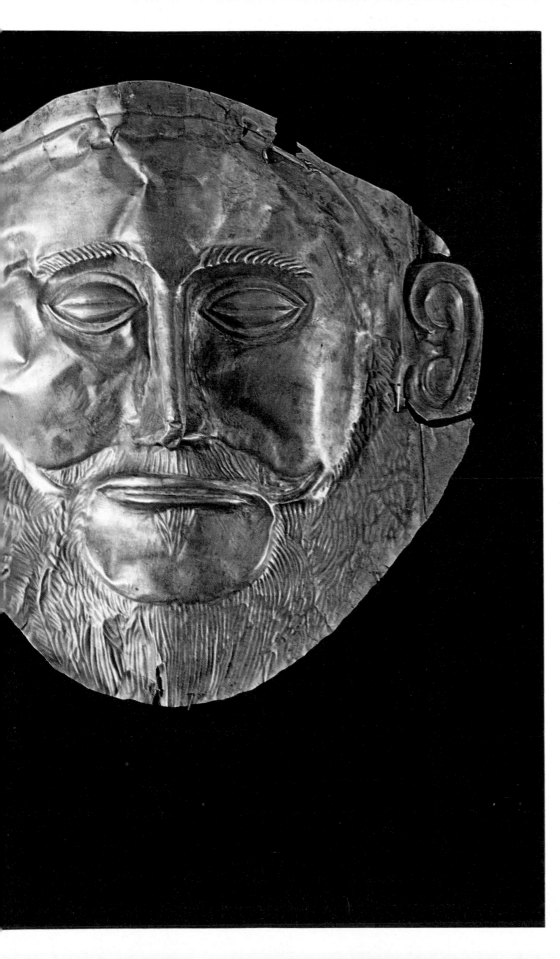

the capture of wild bulls, the other showing tame bulls drawing a plough, also reveal a workmanship closely related to Late Minoan art. The contrast of the scenes – the violence of capture, the peaceful atmosphere of work in the fields – shows a high degree of sensibility; the composition depicts man, animals and natural surroundings in an ensemble of a controlled power to be equalled only much later, in the animal art of the Parthians and the Sassanids.

Archaeologists use the deliberately vague term *kouros* ('boy') to designate the type of male statue most widespread in the Archaic period. The *kouroi* were for a long time thought to represent Apollo, but nowadays it is suggested that they may not

GOLDEN GOBLET FROM MYCENAE (and detail)

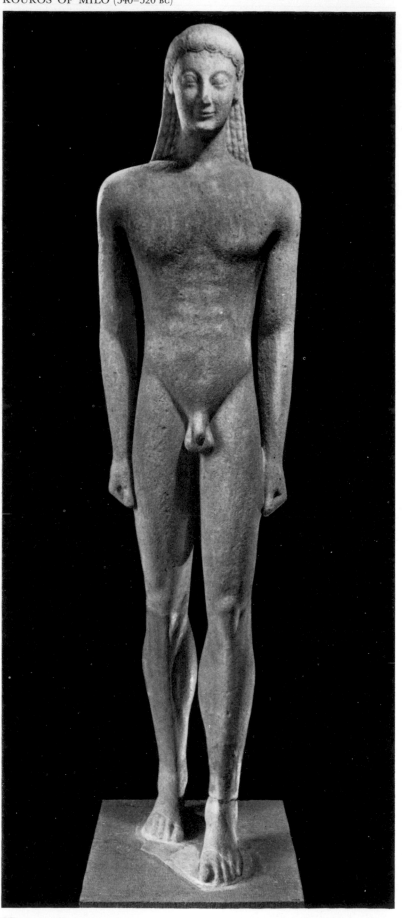

be identifiable either with this god or with any particular figure. They are probably votive or offering statues and a symbolic representation of youthful strength and beauty. This typically Ionian statuary had begun in the seventh century BC with the colossi inspired by Egyptian models and hewn in the marble quarries of Naxos and Paros. At this period Greek merchants had established themselves in the delta of the Nile, founding the city of Naucratis and renewing the links with Egypt which the islands had lost since the Mycenaean empire. Although a certain originality soon appeared in the bronze statuettes of the 'Daedalic' style (Daedalus was the legendary Cretan architect and sculptor supposed to have built the Labyrinth at Knossos and to have possessed the gift of expressing movement in stone), there can be no doubt that the whole of this period was closely dependent on Egyptian aesthetics, notably in its adoption of the frontal principle defined by the archaeologist Lange in 1892: the median plane is always vertical and on each side of this axis the symmetry of the parts is absolute. In the sixth century Greece freed itself from this influence and began to create its own art. The technique of working marble was mastered; the use of the awl and of abrasives made way for carving by chisel. The anatomical details – ears, ribs and muscles – which at first had been treated independently, now blended with the statue as a whole. The Archaic smile, which had originated in Asia and symbolized a divine essence, became more relaxed and natural. A great step had been taken towards realism and if the posture (left foot forward, arms alongside the body) retained the same formalism, it had shed its inhuman rigidity.

After the glorious Cretan civilization and that of Mycenae, which was partially its heir, the Dorian invasion spread three centuries of darkness over Greece (from the twelfth to the eighth centuries). During the early stage of Greek art, the first centres of which were Naxos, Paros and Delos, followed by Samos, Miletus and Rhodes, Eastern art exercised a decisive influence, in Geometric modelling (eighth century), Daedalic modelling (seventh century) and the Archaic modelling of the sixth century. The new artistic awakening, which had come from Ionia and Crete, quickly reached Corinth and the Peloponnesus, but Athens remained isolated from this creative current until the end of the sixth century.

When one observes the *Kouros of Milo*, one realizes that Greece had at last been born. Freed from the Egyptian influence, from the colossal, inhuman art that had emerged from stone and had remained devoted to stone, man had set foot on the earth – he was free and his smile was no longer a convention, but an expression of humanity and benevolence. Here was Greek man with his nobility, his irony, his generosity and his aristocratic tastes, qualities

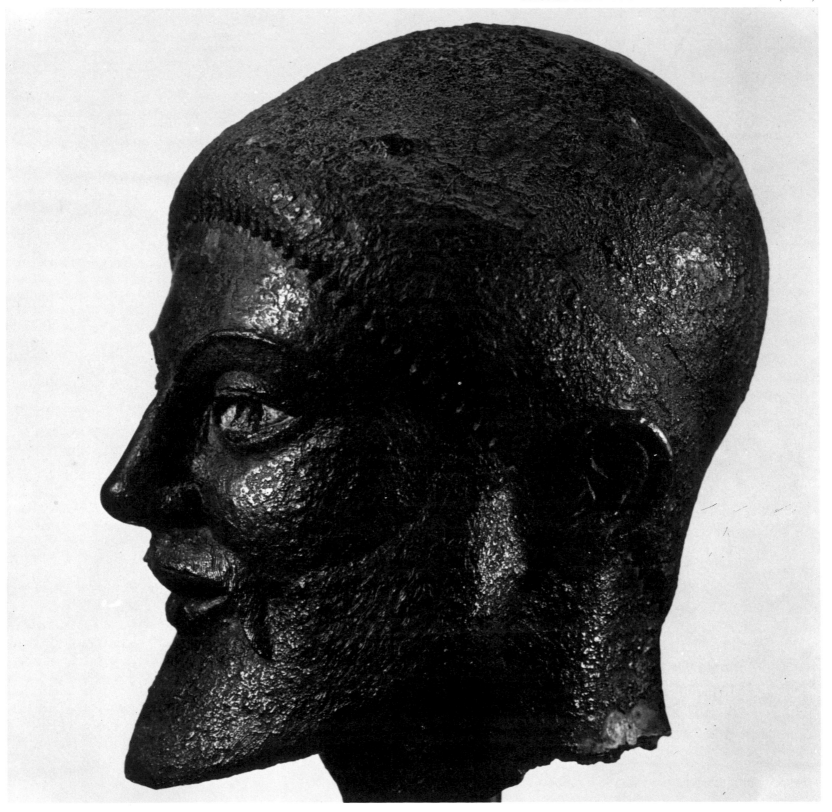

that were to radiate over the Classical epoch and make Athenian democracy possible. Here was man *kallos kagathos,* 'beautiful and good', for virtue and beauty were identical values in Greek ethics.

The funerary stelae are undoubtedly the most sensitive expression of the Classical statuary of the fifth century, to which Phidias and his pupils brought brilliance and glory, but also a rather cold and conventional formalism; the stelae evoke the memory of the deceased with great delicacy and simplicity. The Greeks glorified not only the

31

gods, but also the dignity of the human condition; at the same time, they were conscious of the brevity and futility of life.

Transient being! Who is each one of us?
What is he not?
Man is the dream of a shadow . . .

Although they have a thoroughly Shakespearean resonance, these lines were written by Pindar in the sixth century BC.

In the Classical period corpses were no longer burnt, as they had been in the time of Homer; they were buried in a wood coffin or an earthenware sarcophagus and commemorated with a stone or marble stele. The themes of the carvings which decorate the stelae are touching in their simplicity and in their desire to show the deceased in his daily life: an old man holding out a grasshopper to his dog, a little girl stroking pigeons. The epitaphs are brief and sober; the inscription on a young warrior's tomb reads: 'To the memory of Xenophates, in testimony to his courage and his simplicity, his father Cleobulus has had this monument erected.'

The Greeks had no very definite ideas about life beyond the grave. In the world of the dead, ruled by Hades and guarded by a monstrous dog, Cerberus, they believed that souls were barely conscious shadows who only came to life by drinking blood – 'bats uttering cries in a cave', in Homer's image.

The Athenians of the Golden Age did not fear death when it was a sacrifice offered to the city; they even regarded it as the noble conclusion of their life. With the beginning of the Peloponnesian War in 431 BC, personal ambitions, materialist appetites and social instability were to destroy this heroic conception of death, and the cults of the 'mysteries' – the Eleusinian, Dionysian and Orphic cults – enjoyed great success because they offered more optimistic hopes of a future life. Funerals were conducted

in accordance with a precise ceremonial. The women washed the body, perfumed it and dressed it in white, placing in the mouth of the deceased the obolus intended for Charon, the ferryman of Hades; then the body was laid on a bed at which relatives and friends joined in lamentation. On the evening after the burial, which took place either before sunrise or after sunset, the house was purified and a banquet was given.

At Athens in February the Anthesteria or Festival of the Dead was celebrated; the days of remembrance ended with the prosaic formula: 'Go away, spirits, the Anthesteria are finished.'

At the end of the fifth century BC, statuary began to show a movement and a freedom which contrasted with the severity of the Classical ideal and heralded a new current, originating once again in Ionia, but the emergence of which was partly due to the evolution of Athenian society and its newly-acquired taste for luxury and pleasure. The robust, voluptuous bodies of the Amazons on the pediment of the Temple of Asclepius at Epidaurus express a realism that was to become even more marked, resulting in Asia Minor in the baroque expressionism of Pergamum (third and second centuries BC). These Amazons, whom the heroes Achilles and Theseus had engaged in combat, symbolized the barbarous powers over which Greek civilization had triumphed. Dressed in a short tunic and barebreasted, these horsewomen adorned the pediments and friezes of the temples of the Parthenon, Olympia and Epidaurus.

Bronze, a noble material, was always greatly cherished by Greek artists. In the eighth century there appeared in the Peloponnesus some admirable heads of griffins, serving as handles for cauldrons, and stylized figurines of warriors and animals which possess an immensely comic vitality and undoubtedly owe much

to Mycenaean techniques.

The great bronze statues of the Classical age have mostly vanished, having been transformed into cannons and mortars over the centuries; only a few have miraculously survived, such as the *Charioteer* at Delphi or the *Poseidon* recovered from the bottom of the sea and now in the National Museum at Athens. The statuettes, on the other hand, are sufficiently numerous to reveal a workmanship full of character and invention. These little bronzes have a wonderful firmness, vitality and conciseness; imbued with the tradition of rustic craftsmanship in which the Archaic influence long remained evident, they possess a touching intimacy and sincerity. In the Classical period both statues and statuettes were moulded in a hollow form by the lost wax process; earlier, in the Geometric and Daedalic period, figurines were cast in solid form in individual moulds. The great sculptors are now known chiefly by the fame of certain of their works and by the Roman copies of these. Nothing remains of the sculpture of Polycletus, a citizen of Argos who outshone Phidias as the master of fifth-century statuary. In the case of the leading artists of the fourth century, Myron, Praxiteles and Lysippus, a few of their works are extant, but cannot always be identified with certainty.

Pliny, a man of letters and an enlightened art-lover, after recalling the last works of Lysippus, wrote: *Deinde cessavit ars* ('Then art ceased'), an abrupt and not altogether just conclusion. Admittedly, after the great adventure which it had experienced under Alexander, Greece was to fall into political decline, but on the intellectual and artistic planes the third and second centuries BC were to be a time of passionate emotions, a period of troubles and ferment abroad, of spiritual restlessness and inquiry. It was then that sculpture and, in particular, painting really discovered space, a sense of individuality,

WARRIOR (late 8th century BC)   GIRL RUNNING (Laconian art)   SHEPHERD (6th century BC)

BRONZE STATUETTE OF A HORSEMAN (6th century BC)

PHALLIC STATUETTE

a new kind of sensibility which captured the grace and the fragility of the moment. Painting had always played an important part in Greek art; unfortunately it is difficult to evaluate today, since the original works have been lost almost without trace. It is known, however, that in the fifth century painters such as Polygnotus and Mikon decorated the walls of the public buildings in Athens and Delphi, and that the reputation of Apelles, the painter at the court of Alexander the Great, equalled that of the greatest sculptors. In the Roman copies at Pompeii and Herculaneum, moreover, one can discern the qualities that proclaim the perfection of this art: the sense of rhythm and composition, the feeling for movement, the accurate analysis of posture, the sensitive expression of nature – everything that was to characterize the history of modern painting from the fifteenth to the twentieth centuries is already there in essence. Certain pastoral scenes recall the painting of the Song dynasty in China and the delicate sketches of the French painter Fragonard; the famous mosaic in the Naples museum, *Alexander at the battle of Issus,* a copy of a Greek painting of the third century BC, has the breadth of Delacroix's finest compositions; the pebble mosaics at Pella, the capital of the Macedonian kings, are said to have delighted Pollaiuolo and Michelangelo (the bodies of the hunters fighting the wild animals suggest a vivid impression of physical strength; see p. 163).

To the uninitiated eye the Greek ideal is usually embodied in this Hellenistic art. The *Victory of Samothrace* and the *Venus of Milo* both date from the second century BC, and when Florence discovered Antiquity, it was this late period that influenced its art; for the artists of the Quattrocento the *Laocoon* group, a typically Hellenistic work now in the Vatican Museum, was the most beautiful and instructive of all Greek statues.

Is the philosopher with the piercing eyes, in the photograph opposite, a Stoic or an Epicurean? These two opposing schools of philosophy flourished in Athens from the end of the fourth century BC and, through the work of their disciples, were to have a great influence on Rome. The Stoics, following their founder Zeno, considered that only virtue mattered and that man must be the complete master of himself. Epicurus, a man of sensitive mind and heart, believed that the goal of life should be the pursuit of happiness, a happiness which he sought, however, in self-restraint and the absence of passion. As always with the Greek philosophers, the ethical and moral precepts of the two schools were contained within a system offering a physical explanation of the world: for Zeno, the world was animated by a rational principle, the *logos*; for the Epicureans, it was composed of the interplay of atoms, as propounded by Democritus, a precursor of modern corpuscular and mechanist theories. But perhaps this

philosopher is simply one of the sceptical 'sophists' (*sophistai*), the professional teachers of the art of knowledge and of rhetoric who were both numerous and influential in the fourth century BC. The sophists imparted their ideas to wealthy young men, applying to both institutions and religion a critical spirit that was to help to destroy traditional values without offering anything really new in their place.

Pottery plays a vital part in our knowledge of Greece. Quite apart from its artistic qualities and the fact that it enables us to glimpse something of Hellenic painting, it provides an illustration of the beliefs, the legends and also the daily life of Antiquity. The technique of pottery-making – shaping on the potter's wheel, baking after decoration and often the application of a glaze – varied

little from the Neolithic period to the end of the fourth century BC when, encountering a rival in the bronze industry, it suffered a rapid decline. It must not be forgotten that its function was essentially utilitarian: vessels for carrying and preserving oil (*amphora*), water (*hydria*) and wine (*krater*), and for drinking (*kantharos, skyphos, rython* and in particular the beautiful Athenian cup with two handles). Other objects served more obvious decorative functions, such as the jewel-boxes (*pyxis*) and the delicate *lekythoi*, oil-containers for funeral rites. The elegant modelling and decorative inventiveness of the objects which they manipulated seemed something quite natural to the Greeks, who possessed an innate sense of beauty. If one leaves aside the extraordinary flowering of Cretan pottery, which showed a total freedom and a thoroughly impressionist sensibility, and is described in a later chapter

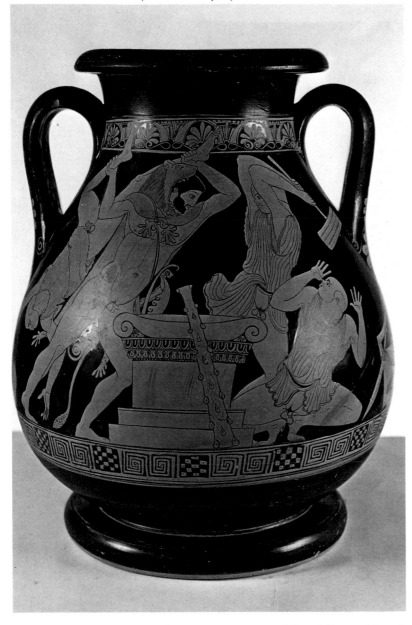

in connection with the museum at Heraklion, Greek pottery can be said to begin with the great vases of the Geometric period (ninth to eighth centuries). Painted in black on a ground of clay, the decoration, at first purely abstract, subsequently displayed a stylization of animals and human beings which gradually became more flexible. An Eastern influence exerted itself in Corinth and Rhodes in the seventh century with motifs reminiscent of Cretan naturalism (flowers, birds, fish, gazelles, lions). The design became more precise, accentuated by incisions and dotted with spots of white, red and sometimes violet. Around 530 BC the Athenians discovered a technique that made for greater clarity, the red figure, which was to guarantee the supremacy of their workshops: the silhouettes were marked with a black line enclosing the red colour of the clay, which was heightened by details painted with the brush and often

by flat tints of colour. In the fifth century a technique was developed by which a white coating capable of taking more delicate gradations of colour was laid over the clay; this polychrome decoration gives an idea of the range of colours employed by the Athenian artists in their frescoes; the technique was used with much grace and subtlety on the funerary vessels (*lekythoi*).

In this decorative art it is the design that catches the eye; it often displays an admirable skill and conciseness, and sometimes a remarkable sensitivity.

The names of certain artists are known: Exekias, Euphronius, Oltus and Epictetus. Others did not sign their works and have been dubbed by scholars with names such as 'Painter of the Niobides' or (which might seem sacrilege to the layman) 'Painter of Berlin', 'Painter of Chicago', and so on.

Against a general background of highly academic subjects (adventures of the gods, exploits of heroes), periods of greater creative originality stand out; never was the narrative character of this art more free or more richly comic than in the late seventh and early sixth centuries BC. The beginning of the fifth century saw the great period of the scenes of banquets and dancing of Brygos and Onesimos, and the end of that century produced some female nudes of a delightful sensuality.

Piraeus is a suburb of Athens whose reputation owes much to a song. Today it is an agglomeration of roughly 400,000 inhabitants, without any real claim to beauty. Only the cafés have retained a local colour; sometimes, to the sound of the *bouzouki* (a small mandolin), a customer inspired by a few glasses of *retsina* will start moving among the tables with a slow rhythm and jerky gestures, in a combination of mime and dance which is the expression of a distinctly melancholy kind of joy. The *zebetiko*, connected with a

secret sect, is of mysterious origin.

In the fifth century BC Piraeus occupied only the peninsula, whose jagged coastline sheltered three harbours, as it still does today: Tourko Limano, a charming spot now reserved for yachts (in Antiquity it was called Munychia and, like its neighbour, Pacha Limani, the ancient Zea, served as a naval dockyard and arsenal); Pacha Limani; and the Main Port, used by the liners and cargo-ships. In the time of the glorious fleet of Salamis, the Main Port, then named Cantharus, already possessed a vast roadstead and well-protected docks.

Today Piraeus is one of the great Mediterranean ports and the enterprising spirit of the Greek shipowners is famous, even if it sometimes hides behind the flag of Panama. In ancient times, however, the maritime role of Athens was not immediately obvious; in the fourth century BC its port of Phalerum was less important than those of Corinth and Aegina. One man, Themistocles, was really responsible for creating the naval power of Athens. He realized that the city needed a large number of warships to defend itself against the menacing expedition of Xerxes. He persuaded the assembly of the people that the construction of these ships should be financed with the proceeds from the rich seams of silver discovered at the mines of Laurium. As Athens lacked sailors, the ships were manned with infantrymen, the *hoplitai*; later, the ungrateful city accused Themistocles of having transformed valorous warriors into vile galley-slaves. Themistocles founded Piraeus, having its docks hollowed out and its arsenals and fortifications built. But his most important achievement was the Long Walls, the two ramparts erected 160 metres apart to protect the military road six kilometres long linking the harbour and the city, which thus assumed a permanent physical and moral unity.

Within a few years, by dint of will-power, imagination and effort, Themistocles had built and armed the 200 triremes which crushed the Persian fleet at Salamis (480 BC). The naval supremacy of Athens, which this victory had demonstrated, was to bring many changes. With Aegina defeated and Corinth eclipsed, Athens could claim to be the protector of the Aegean and gathered islands and cities together in the confederacy of Delos, which the latter entered as allies, though they were quickly reduced to vassals. The embellishments of the Acropolis were financed partly with the revenue collected by the confederation and by a number of punitive expeditions. Above all, its naval hegemony guaranteed Athens not only security of corn supplies, which were vital to the city, but also the opportunity of rapidly becoming the leading commercial city in Hellas; it had the bravest sailors and the most skilful merchants. Xenophon, in his naïve vanity, wrote: 'Throughout Greece and among the Barbarians is there any people capable of enriching itself like the Athenians? If building wood is abundant in one town, or in another iron, copper or flax, how can an outlet be found for this merchandise except by association with the city that rules the seas? We have the ships; without taking anything from the land, we obtain everything by sea.'

Although the importation of cereals was subject to strict regulations, since it was essential for the life of the city, the other branches of commerce were free, except for the imposition of customs duty, and offered fruitful opportunities to the metics and to enterprising citizens. The quays of the harbour and the lanes leading to it, cluttered with merchandise and swarming with a motley crowd, must have been rather like the old districts of Naples or Marseille, their colourful vitality and odours enhanced with the Oriental flavour of souks and bazaars.

The merchant ships were called 'round' or 'hollow' in contrast with the more slender and shallow warships. They relied mainly on sail and the largest had a capacity of 400 tons. They ventured on to the high seas, sometimes over great distances, loading corn in the ports of the Black Sea, Sicily and Egypt. Depending on the hazards of the sea, the cargo of a single ship could mean wealth or ruin for the person chartering it, though it seems that the cunning 'metics' of Piraeus did not allow themselves to be ruined so easily. Like Shakespeare's *The Merchant of Venice*, Aristophanes could well have written a *Merchant of Piraeus*.

When Themistocles was punished by ostracism – that curious institution which made it possible to banish a citizen without trial – Cimon and Pericles continued his work. The philosopher and geometrician Hippodamus of Miletus, the theoretician of geometric town-planning, is supposed to have drawn up at Piraeus the plans of an ideal city of 10,000 inhabitants with straight streets intersecting at right angles.

In the middle of the fifth century BC Athens possessed 400 triremes, the symbols and the instruments of its sea power. The trireme was a ship with three tiers of oars, fifty yards long and about seven yards wide, holding 170 oarsmen and some thirty soldiers. The Athenian navy was particularly expert in the art of boarding enemy vessels. At the head of each ship a *trierarchos*, chosen annually by the *strategoi* from among the wealthiest citizens, was responsible for subsidizing the cost of maintaining the ship of which he held honorary command. The Athenian fleet leaving Piraeus must have been a wonderful sight. Xenophon describes the general enthusiam that greeted the departure of the Sicilian expedition in June 415 BC: 134 triremes and 5,000 picked soldiers (who were never to return). Syracuse, aided by Sparta, crushed the fleet and the army, the greatest disaster in the history of Athens. A few years later (August 405), off Aigospotami, Lysander, commander of the Spartan fleet, captured the Athenian fleet and showed no mercy, massacring all the Athenian prisoners. Then followed the siege of Piraeus, the surrender of Athens and, to the sound of the Spartan flutes, the demolition of the fortifications and the Long Walls, the symbols of the greatness and prosperity of Athens. The misfortunes of Piraeus were not yet over; fearfully devastated by Sulla in 86 BC, it was for a long time hardly more than a village and only came back to life at the beginning of the nineteenth century.

Robert Cohen, in his *History of Greece*, has rightly stressed the supreme importance for Athens of its close and permanent fusion with Piraeus. In this link he sees an essential feature of the Athenian genius and the expression of everything that was best in its democratic ideal: a spirit of fraternity among peasants, workers, sailors and tradesmen, at a time when the other cities had privileged clans – the landowners in Thebes, the military in Sparta and the rich merchants in Corinth.

Except in the summer months when they are occupied almost exclusively by tourists, it is in the little lanes of Plaka, cluttered with the tables of taverns, that one can best capture the zest for life and the brotherly intimacy

which, in spite of their quarrels, the Athenians have always had in common. Admittedly, relationships between Greeks sometimes have a surprisingly 'feudal' character – is this, perhaps, the result of 600 years of Turkish occupation? In Greece, more than in other European countries, the rich seem very rich and the poor very poor. And yet, what warmth of feeling they show to each other, how they enjoy drinking and singing together! This sense of the equality of men, regardless of social inequalities, has long been a peculiar feature of Greece and, paradoxically, it is economic and social progress that is putting this ideal in jeopardy. In Greece, in the villages and the ports, the people of the most modest social background are often the most dignified and generous; but here, as in other countries, the blind craving for money and comfort is destroying the virtues of heart and mind, replacing them with envy, vanity and bad taste. Yet there is no need to be too pessimistic; it is not so long ago that Henry Miller made his joyful discovery of Greece and wrote in *The Colossus of Maroussi*: 'For the first time in my life, too, I had met men who were like men ought to be – that is to say, open, frank, natural, spontaneous, warm-hearted.' There are still many Greeks of this kind, as there were in ancient times.

In the fifth century BC Athens had a population of about 400,000: 40,000 'citizens' and 20,000 'metics' or aliens, with their wives and children, formed a half of the population; the other half consisted of slaves. Athens was not a slave city in the same sense as certain cities of Asia Minor, or Rome in later years. Most families had two or three slaves, who were occupied in domestic tasks; the wealthiest citizens had more, sometimes over fifty, employed on their estates or in their mills. There were also public slaves who occupied minor offices, receiving a wage and living wherever they chose. The Athenians had a reputation for being kind to their slaves, who were protected by laws; many slaves played a full part in family life, joining in prayers and celebrations, and were even buried beside their masters. But some led a wretched existence, turning mill-wheels or working in the silver-mines of Laurium, where over 10,000 of them were employed.

Here is a brief portrait of a typical citizen of Athens. First of all, he was a 'citizen' because his father had been born in Athens. In 451 BC Pericles issued a decree making it obligatory for the mother also to be Athenian by birth. The young citizen would be eligible to participate in the assembly of the people (*ecclesia*) after his military service – that is, after having been an *ephebos* ('youth') from the ages of eighteen to twenty. He would marry late, at about the age of thirty-five, taking a fifteen-year-old girl as his wife. Like everyone else, he would dress in a garment of wool or flax (the *himation*), a short under-tunic (the *chiton*) and a cap (the *pilos*). He would wash rarely; when necessary, he would wipe his hands in his hair, which he wore short. He was frugal in his eating habits (cakes of wheat or barley, onions, beans or lentils, cheese, sometimes fish and, more rarely, chicken, pork or goat-meat). He was not often at home. He might be the owner of an oil-mill with five slaves working for him. Occasionally, with a few friends, he would organize a *symposion*, a drinking bout enlivened by female flute-players who were usually not over-shy. He had no family worries; his son was entrusted to a slave, the *paidagogos*, who would take the boy to the schoolmaster, with whom he would read Homer and learn music, and to the wrestling school (*palaistra*), where he would exercize his body. Above all, the Athenian citizen loved his city and was ready to die for it. Attending all the assemblies, he would eventually be appointed a juror (*heliastes*) and a senator (*bouleutes*), by the drawing of lots. He showed no pity to his enemies and was highly sensitive about his honour. He loved courage, beauty, simplicity and moderation. He preferred poetry, metaphor and feeling to abstract ideas. For him, wisdom (*sophia*) meant doing well whatever he undertook. He was happy and proud to be a free citizen of the leading city of Hellas – the Hellas which he knew to be so manifestly superior to the servile multitudes of Egypt and Asia.

This is a sketch of an Athenian citizen of the period from the sixth to the middle of the fifth century BC. The Peloponnesian War soon brought far-reaching changes. Thucydides denounced the corruption, tyranny, violence and demagogy rampant everywhere; indignantly he declared that now only private self-interest mattered. In the time of Demosthenes, in spite of the orator's exhortations, the citizens of Athens were no longer willing to fight in defence of their city, preferring to call on mercenaries. This abrupt decline of Athenian 'virtue' stemmed from a radical change of economic and social equilibrium: the enrichment of a few and the impoverishment of the rest had resulted in the demise of the middle class on which Athenian democracy had depended. Precariously balanced between the necessity of public order and the exigences of individual liberty, democracy was to suffer, with the arrival of Alcibiades and factions of ambitious men, the ordeals of demagogy and then anarchy.

Some sensitive souls are filled with indignation by the cruelty of the Athenians, who massacred their prisoners, or at best reduced them to slavery, and abandoned their new-born daughters at street-corners; others praise their cult of beauty and their sublime humanism. As Ezra Pound might have said, this is 'a quarrel by jackals around a dried-up well'. In a few hundred years from now the crimes committed by the Greeks will seem no more surprising than certain practices of the nineteenth century – sending children to work in mills, for instance – or of the police-states and military regimes of the twentieth century. Circumscribed by their historical context, civilizations do not perform miracles; they make efforts and achieve progress. To speak of the 'Greek miracle' is only meaningful as an image of the extraordinary flowering of man which took place in Greece, a phenomenon which, with the exception of the Italian Renaissance, was never to be equalled in the West. Man did not originate in Greece, but it was there that he first became truly conscious of his condition and gave a form to the ideas and sentiments which have never ceased to inspire him throughout the vicissitudes of history. It is worth listening to the poets of Hellas – they speak of the Greeks, but they also speak of ourselves:

> *When youth has gone,*
> *Taking with it vain follies,*
> *Who can ever free himself,*
> *Bowed beneath a thousand memories?*

These lines lamenting the transience of life's joys sound like François Villon, but were written by Sophocles. The Greeks accepted their human condition with a lucid resignation. Earlier, Homer had observed:
Such is the destiny that the gods have woven for unfortunate mortals,
To live in grief, while they are free from troubles . . .
Injustice is not only the gods' doing, but also that of men:

> *In the chorus not everyone sings.*
> *Many are silent and the last rows*
> *Have been put there to make up the number.*
> *The poor merely make an appearance,*
> *Only those who have money are truly alive.*

Menander

Without illusions about his future destiny, man can be satisfied if he fulfils himself in his *aretē* – that is, in all his talents:

> *Do not believe, my dear soul, in eternal life,*
> *but exhaust the field of the possible!*

Pindar

In their daily life the Greeks had principles like ourselves, principles which, if one is to judge by Aristophanes, young people readily derided, as they do today:
You will learn not to answer your father back, not to call him greybeard, not to blame him for his age and for the time when he used to lift you up like a chicken.

It is said that the Greeks had little affection for their wives and children. The question put to Critobulus by Socrates is often quoted: 'Are there persons with whom you have less conversation than with your wife?' To which Critobulus replied: 'If there are, there are few.' But the reply is ageless and could well be made by many husbands of today.

Is there, on the other hand, a confession more moving than that made by the mother of Ulysses to her son who came to see her in Hades?
It is my longing and concern for you, my dear child,
It is the tenderness I feel for you that has robbed me of the honeyed

taste of life . . .
And Euripides puts these heart-felt words into the mouth of Andromache:

> *Our children are our soul.*
> *He who has none suffers less grief,*
> *But his happiness is a melancholy thing.*

It is also said that, apart from masculine friendships, the Greeks showed few feelings; and yet, has the love of man and woman ever been more beautifully evoked than by Apollonius of Rhodes describing Medea and Jason?
They were like great oaks or pines
Which have taken root, calm and side by side, on the mountainside,
When the wind subsides; but if the wind suddenly blows up,
Then the trees toss, resounding into the distance.
And so they both would go to be with each other under the breath of
Love.

Certainly, the majority of Greek men liked drinking bouts, courtesans and little boys, but they also loved Homer, the theatre and music.

> *Life is pleasure or nothing.*
> *The life of men is short. Come then! Wine*
> *And dancing and flowers and women . . .*

writes a Hellenistic poet; at least he did not forget the flowers . . .

The greatness of Greek civilization was to give a form to the highest aspiration of man – for the first time he became truly aware of his condition, revealing his need of self-fulfilment and his longing to reach beyond himself.

Six centuries before Jesus Christ, the philospher Xenophanes wrote of 'a single God, the lord of men and of the gods, whose spirit and nature cannot be compared with those of men'.

And the cry of Antigone – *I was born for love and not for hatred!* – and that of Prometheus – *I would rather be bound like a slave to this rock than see myself transformed into a faithful servant of your all-powerful God!* – called humanity to the twin summits of life: Love and Freedom.

As you leave Athens for Cape Sounion, seventy kilometres away, you first take the motorway that runs along the sea; when you have passed the aerodrome, a narrower and less busy road follows the twists and turns of the coastline. To the left rises the grey mass of Mount Hymettus, which assumes a softer, golden hue at sunrise and sunset. This mountain range encloses Athens to the east; in spite of its desert-like appearance, it has hidden oases of cypresses and laurels; its slopes, covered with aromatic plants (thyme, turpentine, sage, mint and lavender), have made the reputation of the honey that bears its name – judging by the labels on the jars, all the bees of Greece must gather on Hymettus!

The columns of the Temple of Poseidon on **Cape Sounion** stand on the highest cliff at the farthermost tip of the Greek continent. Below lies the sea. It seems inevit-

iodine, have acquired the dazzling crystalline appearance of salt. On the other side of the peninsula Lavrion, the ancient Laurion or Laurium famous for its rich deposits of silver, now produces calamine (zinc) and manganese. This desolate spot seems still to bear witness to the miserable fate of the thousands of slaves who worked the mines in Antiquity.

Chateaubriand, on his way to Jerusalem, visited Sounion: 'In the distance I saw the sea of the Archipelago with all its islands; the setting sun reddened the slopes of Zea and the fourteen beautiful columns of white marble below which I was sitting. The sage and the junipers spread an aromatic odour round the ruins, and the noise of the waves barely reached me . . .' The quotation is best left unfinished, for the rest is like syrup. It is indeed astounding that this writer, one of the greatest in the French language, with his prodigious eye and his biting wit in the analysis and description of men and events, should have succumbed to facile landscape-painting in the Romantic manner. How much more moving and evocative than these empty, artificial phrases are the brief and dazzling images of Homer: 'the waves with their countless smiles' and 'the cyclone of dust which the horses' hooves lift into the sky'.

One day, at this extremity of Attica, a fabulous armada from Asia appeared: 1,200 steel-clad ships, decorated with gold and leather and powerfully armed. Xerxes, emperor of Persia, had set off to conquer the Greek world ten years after his father Darius. The fleet was never to return past Cape Sounion, for it was destroyed off the island of Salamis in what was perhaps the most glorious hour of Greek history, when courage and unity prevailed. The account which Herodotus gives of this heroic battle should be read, with its terrible picture of the end of the day and the Greeks dispatching the Persians who had fallen into the sea, spearing them like fish.

able that Poseidon, god of the sea, should have been worshipped here. The temple, associated with the smaller temple of Athena, was des-

troyed by the Persians and rebuilt during the time of Pericles; the fifteen remaining Doric columns, battered by the wind from the sea and eroded by

2 Delphi and the Peloponnesus

Starting on a week's tour of the principal sacred places of Greece – Delphi, Olympia and Epidaurus – the visitor must make sure of stopping at Eleusis. This sanctuary, which played an essential part in the life of the Athenians, especially from the beginning of the Classical period, lies twenty kilometres from the capital, to which it was linked by the Sacred Way. The cult of the Great Goddesses Demeter and Corē (Persephone) continued until the end of the fourth century AD; it was prohibited by the Christian emperor Theodosius shortly after Eleusis had been devastated by Alaric and the Goths. Even if the debris scattered over the ground gives little idea of the renown of the 'mysteries', and even if the industrial surroundings partly spoil the wonderful view of the Bay of Salamis that one could have from this high spot, it is well worth sitting on one of the old stones and allowing the imagination to wander a little. Here the Athenians demonstrated a fraternity that was open to all men; here they experienced the illumination and the certitude of a future life, taking part in mystical 'happenings' which brought them joy and a new hope.

Eleusis, the name of which means 'the arrival', has its origins in mythology. It was here that Demeter received the hospitality of King Celeus after roaming the world in search of her daughter Persephone, who had been carried off by Hades, god of the underworld. Zeus, touched by the goddess's distress (he was Persephone's father), sent Hermes to Hades, his brother; Hades agreed to let Persephone, also known more simply as Corē ('daughter'), return to her mother, but first made her eat some pomegranate seeds; henceforth Corē, bound by a spell, was to come back each year to spend the autumn and winter with her husband in the underworld, returning to earth in the spring when nature awakened. To reward those who had received and helped her in her grief, Demeter presented Triptolemus, son of King Celeus, with an ear of corn whose cultivation would transform the life of mankind; she also initiated two families to the rites of the mysteries, 'august rites which cannot be transgressed, penetrated or divulged', but which brought joy and hope. This cult was undoubtedly inherited from the Cretan and Mycenaean civilizations, many traces of which are to be found at Eleusis. Demeter was a new aspect of the mother-goddess, the symbol of fertility and fecundity as represented by primitive idols like the Indian god Siva, but more peacefully. She also embodied the cosmic force, the vital impulse of nature and of man. In the supernatural atmosphere of the Eleusinian mysteries this symbolism of creation and of the eternal rebirth assumed a mystical form. Although the exact nature of the mystic revelation is not known, the calender of the ceremonial involved has been established. The Great Mysteries of Eleusis were celebrated in September (*boedromion*). All were admitted to the initiation, Barbarians as well as Athenians, slaves as well as freemen, provided that they had received a preliminary instruction given in the spring at Agora, near Athens, on the banks of the river Ilissus; the candidates or *mystai* were purified in the waters of the river. On 13 and 14 *boedromion* the *ephebes* (young men aged 18–20) carried the relics (*hiera*) from Eleusis to Athens; it is thought that the mystical basket contained male and female sexual attributes of clay. On the 15th the candidates were assembled for initiation; the only ones not admitted were 'those whose hands are not pure and whose voice is unintelligible' – that is to say, criminals and foreigners who did not speak Greek. On the 16th the *mystai* went to Phalerum for a curious purification ceremony in which they were required to run towards the sea dragging a young pig, which was then sacrificed. On the 19th a great procession made its way to Eleusis along the Sacred Way, carrying the mystical basket with singing and cries of 'Iacchus! Iacchus!' An *ephebos* represented Dionysus, the young god of joy and love and also, from the late fifth century BC, the god of the dead whose survival he guaranteed (in this new capacity Dionysus sometimes replaced Hades as the husband of Persephone). This long march interrupted by halts doubtless symbolized the path of life, and only Eleusis, 'the arrival', opened the gates of the world beyond. On the nights of the 21st and 22nd the initiation proper took place in the Telesterion, a large square hall where the tiers of seats could accommodate three thousand people in the time of Pericles. The fragments of information available on these ceremonies are contradictory and not at all clear. The first evening (the

21st), it seems, was reserved for the *mystai*, who had to recite the sacred formula: 'I have fasted, I have drunk the *kykeon* [the ritual beverage], I have taken the object from the basket and, after performing the act, I have put it in the pannier, then from the pannier back into the basket.' Were these erotic practices inherited from ealier cults? It is difficult to say, but within the walls of the Telesterion there was certainly some kind of collective emotional experience during the sacred drama recalling the abduction of Persephone and Demeter's frantic search for her. An ancient author speaks of 'anxious, endless marches through the shadows', of 'terror', 'shuddering', 'trembling', 'cold sweat', 'extreme fear' and suddenly, no doubt when Demeter found her daughter and hundreds of torches were lit, a 'wonderful light', 'pure places', 'meadows resounding with song', 'sacred words', 'divine apparitions' and 'joyous men finally free who celebrate the mysteries with crowns on their heads'.

The second night was reserved for the initiates of the previous year, who became *epoptai* ('contemplatives') and thereby reached the highest degree of initiation. It seems that the object unveiled and presented by the *hierophantes* ('the one who shows the sacred things') was an ear of corn, the symbol of fertility and eternal life; the *epoptai* had previously watched another sacred drama in which, it is thought, the union of Zeus and Demeter was mimed by the hierophant and a priestess.

The mysteries were of the utmost importance to leading Greek poets and thinkers such as Hesiod, Pindar, Aeschylus and Plato, and were obviously not simply occasions of religious hysteria. Under an esoteric form they contained a message, and the hopes of a life-after-death which they offered must have entailed certain moral commandments. That only the initiated could attain happiness was the opinion of Sophocles and of many others: 'O thrice happy those mortals who, after contemplating these mysteries, will enter the dwelling of Hades; only they will possess life there; for the rest there will be nothing but suffering.'

The myth of Demeter and Corē, which explains the seasons of the year, is a clear illustration of the Greeks' fondness for legends and images; combining intelligence with sensibility, they gave a poetic form to that which they could not understand. Some critical minds, aware that many things escaped the comprehension of man, probably did not believe in these beautiful stories, but they accepted them nonetheless – like a child with a fairy-tale, they found in them a taste of happiness. The Greeks used this same power of imagination to populate Olympus. The gods which they made in their own image derived from a variety of sources: Zeus, the god of the skies of the Indo-Europeans; Aphrodite, the Phoenician Urania, the ancient fertility-goddess of the Aegean peoples; Artemis, whose originally Oriental character points to her Asiatic antecedents; and Dionysus, a god of a complex nature who appears to have originated in Thrace. The heroes, Hercules, Theseus and Jason, provided a bridge between men and gods. The Greeks were conscious of a higher essence, of the possibilities of achievement which they must realize. They lived in intimate familiarity with these myths, with these gods and heroes, endowed like them with a passionate zest for life. When the philosophers and the sophists began to mock these childish fantasies, when the élite abandoned them and the reign of reason and abstraction arrived, Greece entered upon its decline. This was the end of collective action and the beginning of personal adventure; the admirable precept of Socrates, 'Know yourself', was to lead some to anguish and a guilty conscience, and others to ambition and self-interest. Admittedly, the vindictive gods of Greek religion had not seemed much concerned with good and evil; for them, as for the Greeks, virtue was devotion to the tribe and the city, it was courage, strength, skill and intelligence. What is the use of morality when hearts are pure? To suppress violence and encourage love? But are men more capable of loving merely because they talk and think of love? Do they not love more when they are simply happy?

Between Eleusis and Livadia you pass through the district of Boeotia, a fertile plain surrounded by mountains whose passes provided invaders from the north with access to Attica and the Peloponnesus. Consequently, some of the most famous battles of ancient times were fought on this territory. At the pass of Thermopylae, in 480 BC, the Spartan general Leonidas sacrificed himself and a thousand of his soldiers in an attempt to contain the huge army of Xerxes; attacked from the rear after an act of treachery, the entire Greek force perished after fighting, says Herodotus, 'with sword, hands and teeth'. A few months later, the defeat of the Persians at Plataea (479 BC), following on the naval disaster they had suffered at Salamis, compelled them to return to their own country and gave Greece a glory which it was later to abuse. It was then that the Athenian democracy began to pursue its aggressive policy of expansion. A century and a half later, the victory of Philip II of Macedon over the Athenians and Thebans at Chaeronea (338 BC) gave him access to Greece and enabled him to establish himself as its undisputed master. During the battle the young Alexander annihilated the celebrated 'sacred battalion' of Thebes which thirty years earlier under the command of Pelopidas and Epaminondas had distinguished itself at Leuctra, not far away, by crushing the Spartan army at that time considered invincible. A white marble lion, carved in a proud attitude, bears witness to the sacrifice made by these warriors in a belated attempt to defend the liberty of Greece.

In the Mycenaean period Boeotia enjoyed much greater activity than Attica, and it was at this time that the great myths inherited by Greece must have taken shape here. Hercules (Heracles), the most popular of the Greek heroes, is supposed to have been born here from the union of Zeus and Alcmena, queen of Thebes. An athlete of exemplary courage, a giant capable of both meekness and ferocity, and between exploits a great debaucher of girls, Hercules accomplished the twelve labours which he was set: he strangled the Nemean lion in his own arms, cut off the innumerable heads of the Lernean hydra, cleaned out the stables of Augeas, king of Elis, in a single day, travelled to the end of the world to fetch the golden apples from the garden of the Hesperides, and so on. In spite of the tragic end attributed to him – he was supposed to have had himself burnt on a bonfire after killing his children in a fit of madness – Hercules was regarded by the ordinary people of Greece as their 'champion', while for the artists and poets his countless adventures, his love of Omphale, his dispute with Apollo concerning the Delphic tripod, offered subjects to which they could apply their talents and imagination.

The Oedipus myth represents tragedy of a different kind, the fatality of destiny which sometimes crushes man. In the mournful, monotonous scenery of the Boeotian plain the visitor can almost discover an echo of this imaginary hero. At the crossroads of Megas, Oedipus killed a stranger who had been threatening him; the man was his father, King Laius, whom he had not recognized for the boy had been brought up far from home. On the maps, not far from Thebes, is the name of a village: Sphinx. Was this the site of the crossroads where this strange monster lay in wait for her victims and before devouring them put her riddle to them: What creature walks on all fours in the morning, on two legs during the day and on three in the evening? Oedipus realized that the answer was man in the three stages of his life – childhood, maturity and old age – and the Sphinx, in anger, threw herself into a chasm. Oedipus married Jocasta and became king of Thebes; then plague struck the city; in the course of the investigations made by Oedipus, and which Sophocles describes in the manner of a detective story, he discovered the terrible truth: he had killed his father and married his mother. Today this might not seem such a dreadful thing but Oedipus gouged out his eyes and took to the roads with his daughter, the young Antigone, whose troubles had only just begun.

The Athenians despised the Boeotians, calling them peasants and blockheads, and their scorn has survived to the present time in the rather precious use of the term 'Boeotian' to denote a lack of sensitivity and refinement. It is true that by comparison with its neighbour Attica, Boeotia an agricultural region isolated by its mountains, deprived of outlets to the sea and governed by an oligarchy of rich landowners, played little part in Greek history, and it also drew opprobrium upon itself by its betrayal of the Hellenic cause at the time of the Persian invasion. Yet Boeotia presented a unique example of a confederation of cities and villages each of which respected the equal rights of the rest, an example that could have served as a model for the whole of Greece and averted many of her upheavals. After the fall of Athens, it enjoyed its hour of military glory, repudiating the hegemony of Sparta and defeating the supposedly invincible Spartan armies by the courage of its horsemen and its famous 'sacred battalion', and in particular by employing a new tactic, the attack in oblique order, applied by a leader of genius, Epaminondas. But this success was short-lived; on the disappearance of its two great men, Pelopidas and Epaminondas, who were glorified by Cicero and Plutarch, Thebes was unable to resist Macedonian pressure. The city was conquered and totally destroyed by Alexander in 336 BC.

Nothing remains of ancient 'Thebes with its rich chariots'; but, in order not to be too unjust to Boeotia as one crosses the vast marshland of Copais, now dried up and used for growing cotton, it should be remembered that delicate funerary figurines were modelled in terracotta by the craftsmen of the village of Tanagra (although many statuettes have been wrongly attributed to Tanagra). And one should not forget the songs of Hesiod and Pindar, both natives of Boeotia, or the slopes of Mount Helicon, sacred to the Muses and possessing the fountain of Hippocrene, which was to become a rather hackneyed source of inspiration for certain French poets of the nineteenth century.

At the crossroads of Megas, the scene of the fatal encounter between Oedipus and his father, you come to the junction of the routes that led from Delphi to Thebes, Daulis and Ambrysus (now Distimo). About ten kilometres from Distimo, in a wild and majestic setting, is the **Monastery of Hosios Levkas.** Though founded in the tenth century AD by the holy hermit Levkas, the monastery and its two churches date mostly from the eleventh century. With its beautiful mosaics, its polychrome marble paving and its eighteenth-century paintings, the larger church has an austere grace. The monastery radiates a poetic simplicity which makes a detour well worthwhile.

As soon as Mount Parnassus appears, one enters into a new dimension. These bare, rugged mountain slopes proclaim the sublime and in ancient times were sacred to Apollo, Dionysus and his frantic female companions, the Bacchantes. From Arachova to the approaches of Delphi, nature presents a spectacle of such dramatic intensity that one is left breathless.

Encircled by high cliffs, with a rocky spur concealing the steep descent towards the plain of Itea and its sea of olive-trees, and dominated by the two huge rocks called the Phaedriades ('the brilliant ones') between which gushes the water that fed the sacred Castalian Spring, **Delphi** clings to the mountainside, its ruins arranged like the tiers of some magnificent theatre. Delphi is often said to have an oppressive atmosphere and on a stormy day the scenery can certainly take on a fantastic, almost terrifying appearance; but in the sun it is simply majestic. Although this place gives the impression of having existed since time immemorial – earthquakes and their kaleidoscopic effects have merely intensified its dramatic power – the excavation of the ruins of the sanctuary dates only from the end of the last century, when the French Parliament voted the money for the expropriation

of the village of Kastri and its reconstruction to the west of the excavation site, on which its houses stood. As a result of the work done by the French School of Athens over nearly a century, the visitor of today can discover in the stones of Delphi the testimony of man's presence, the expression of his feelings of fear and reverence, and of his determination to be second to none in the beauty and richness of his offerings to the gods.

According to legend, Zeus had sent two eagles from the extremities of the earth, which the ancients believed to be in the form of a disk, and the eagles met at Delphi above the *omphalos* ('navel', i.e. centre of the earth), a sacred stone that was subsequently placed in the Temple of Apollo.

This wild valley where, as one writer has said, the vibrations of the universe converge, where everything – earth, air, water, fire – is a sign and an omen, was a place of worship and oracular revelation from early times. Probably from the Minoan age, and certainly in the Mycenaean

period, Gaea, the goddess of the earth and fertility, was venerated here, no doubt together with her daughter Themis, and guarded by Python, a female serpent; the cult bore a close resemblance to that of the mother-goddess of the Cretans. The sanctuary was then named Pytho – 'Pytho the rocky' in the words of Homer. Apollo Delphinos, the island god worshipped by the Cretan sailors in the form of a dolphin (*delphis*), killed the serpent and took possession of the sacred stone and of the famous tripod, on which he installed a priestess, the Pythia, whom he instructed to transmit his messages (a benevolent god, he had decided to act as interpreter between his father, Zeus, and mankind, whose lot he strove to alleviate). The cult of Apollo appears to have been established at Delphi at the beginning of the eighth century BC. The sanctuary which enjoyed the protection of the Amphictyonic Council (the association of the twelve surrounding states) soon became the most renowned in Greece. Its Pan-Hellenic role

was revealed in the games held at Delphi every four years and, above all, in the fame of its oracle which was consulted by all the cities of Hellas, by the princes of Asia, the kings of Egypt and later by the emperors of Rome. The Greeks wanted to know the will of the gods, the destiny awaiting them, perhaps so that they might prepare themselves, but more probably in the hope of averting a sinister fate; divination therefore played an important part in their religion. They used various methods, borrowed no doubt from the ancient practices of each different nation: the future was read in the noise of oak-leaves, in the flight of birds, or in the livers of sacrificed animals; but Delphi enjoyed a supreme privilege, for here the gods could be questioned through the mediation of the Pythia.

The Pythia, often a simple country girl, uttered the 'truthful' and 'infallible' oracles of Apollo in the most remote part of the temple, probably underground, the *adyton* ('the place to which there is no access'). Near her were the gold statue of Apollo, the tomb of Dionysus, his

beloved brother who was often associated with his cult, and the *omphalos*, the 'navel of the earth'. The priests could not see her but could hear her words, passing on her reply to the consultant; the answer, always expressed in an obscure form, had to be interpreted by qualified persons (*exegetai*). There are two opposing schools of thought concerning the exact nature of the Pythia's inspiration. In the opinion of some she delivered the oracle in a state of trance or delirium induced by sulphurous exhalations, a view supported by the texts of Latin authors such as Lucian, Cicero and Plutarch. Others attributing more dignity to the cult evoke a Pythia of calm and noble demeanour who, after purifying herself with the water of the Castalian Spring and chewing a laurel-leaf, uttered the divine message with a branch in her hand.

The oracles of the Pythia had a powerful moral, religious and political influence especially during the periods of deep faith – the seventh, sixth and the first half of the fifth centuries, before the appearance of the sophists and of a certain scepticism in Greek religious life. In the fourth century Plato still makes the sanctuary the religious pivot of his ideal republic: 'It is Apollo, the god of Delphi, who should dictate the most important, the most beautiful and the first of the laws, those concerning the founding of temples, sacrifices and the cult of the gods in general.' Yet the opportunism of the Delphic priests was often evident; at the time of the invasion of Xerxes in 480 BC the envoys of the great king seem to have been well received; the Pythia warned the Athenians of dreadful calamities and the Amphictyonic Council, Boeotia included, joined the Persian camp. After the Greek victory the interpretation of the oracle was modified and the offerings of the victors came pouring in. Thereafter, however, the political subordination of the sanctuary became obvious and the oracle served as the mouthpiece of whichever state happened to be dominant: Athens, then Sparta, Thebes and Macedonia. At the request of the Amphictyonic Council, Philip II intervened at Delphi to subdue the Phocians and soon

occupied the whole of Greece.

The Temple of Apollo nevertheless seems to have played a major role in the evolution of Greek thought, lessening fatalism, tempering the rigour of Greek laws with compassion, and combating violence and vengeance, the two scourges of Greece. The *Oresteia* of Aeschylus expresses vividly the 'humanist' message of the god of poetry,

music and the sciences. With what violence and indignation Apollo drives the Erinyes, the bloodstained hounds of vengeance, from his sanctuary! 'Do not come near this dwelling! Your place is where heads are chopped off and eyes torn out, where throats are cut and children are robbed of the flower of their youth.' And Pindar glorified Apollo as 'he who brings to

men and women the remedies that heal their cruel sufferings, he who fills hearts with love and harmony and with hatred of civil war'.

When visiting Delphi it is well worthwhile consulting Pausanias, the great traveller of the second century AD, who wrote a lively and excellently documented 'guide-book' entitled *Periegesis* ('Itinerary') *of Greece* a trans-

Pausanias, one should begin a visit with the first remnants of the sanctuary which come into sight as one approaches Delphi from Arachova, below the road. At the site called Marmaria, on a terrace surrounded by a forest of olive-trees, lie the temples of Athena Pronaia (*pronaia* meaning 'guardian of the temple'); first you find the traces of the ancient Doric temple built of tufa in the sixth century; after its destruction by a landslide in the fifth century, a new temple of limestone was erected to the west, in a less exposed position. Between the two temples are the ruins of two treasuries – that in the Ionic style is believed to have been built by the Greeks of Massilia (Marseille) – and

hundred-year-old olive trees and leading to the gymnasium, occupying two terraces and largely rebuilt by the Romans. The gymnasium comprised a track as long as that of the stadium, a wrestling-school (*palaistra*) and baths; it was not restricted to the training of athletes, for astronomy was also practised under its colonnade.

If you go back to the road and walk a short way along it as far as the first bend, you will see the celebrated Castalian Spring; a basin cut out of the rock receives the water that trickles from the bottom of the crevice separating the two huge rocks called the Phaedriades. Sheltered by plane trees, this spot is ideal for day-dreaming – if you happen to find yourself alone,

lation of which can be bought at your local bookshop. Even if he knew the institutions of Greece only in their decadent phase, Pausanias is an invaluable companion for the buildings now scattered in fragments over the ground were still standing in his time and his descriptions stimulate the imagination without detracting from the poetic effect of the ruins. Like

the wonderful *tholos*, a white marble rotunda erected in the fourth century with stunning grace and delicacy, but the function of which is unknown (several pieces of its frieze are displayed in the museum); three of the twenty columns of its peristyle have been re-erected and provide one of Delphi's most stirring sights. Leaving the Marmaria site, you follow a path shaded by

which would be something of a miracle! In the tourist season Delphi seems to become the rallying-point for all the motor coaches in Greece, and if the tourists appear like swarms of multi-coloured little ants against this gigantic background, they rarely show the ant's virtues of silence and discretion. Sometimes, however, in the spring or autumn, one can experience a sublime

flaunted their power and prosperity. The treasuries of the Sicyonians, the Siphnians, the Thebans, the Boeotians, the Athenians, the Cnidians and the Corinthians, the *ex-voto* offerings of the Lacedaemonians, the kings of Argos, the princes of Pergamum, the tyrants of Syracuse and the kings of Lydia, wove a garland of unparalleled opulence round the Temple of Apollo. Herodotus mentions the fabulous gifts presented to the sanctuary by Croesus, king of Lydia (more than ten tons of gold). Near the temple, four tripods donated by Gelon, tyrant of Syracuse, after he had defeated the Carthaginians (480 BC), supported gold figures of Victories weighing about fifty talents (about one and a half tons).

In this mighty exhibition of sacred art the Greek cities gave full vent to their rivalries; there were disputes about sites, which were often chosen with a view to insulting another city and paying off old scores. If the Athenians celebrated the victory of Salamis with a magnificent portico, Sparta in its turn felt obliged to demonstrate in stone the importance of its role in the defeat of the Persians. When the Lacedaemonians under Lysander had vanquished the Athenian fleet at Aigospotami (405 BC), they erected the monument of the *Nauarchoi* ('admirals'). Beaten in their turn at Leuctra (371), they saw the Boeotians and Arcadians place statues of their own heroes near the monument to spite them. After the disaster suffered by Nicias's expedition to Sicily, Syracuse took pleasure in building its treasury opposite that of the Athenians.

At the first bend of the Sacred Way stands the Treasury of the Athenians, re-erected in 1903 and dating from the early fifth century BC, a structure in the Doric style of perfect grace and sobriety. Most of its metopes, which depict the exploits of Hercules and Theseus, are in the museum which also contains some interesting fragments from the two neighbouring treasuries: that of the Sicyonians (sixth century), with metopes of Archaic workmanship, and that of the Siphnians, with a pediment and frieze of an intensely lifelike quality which are typical of the Oriental character of Ionic art in the sixth century. The combat of warriors and lions reproduced on the inside covers of this book is a striking example of the calm strength of this epic style. In the museum you will also find the winged sphinx from the Naxian Column (sixth century), one of the many marble *ex-voto* monuments that stood along the Sacred Way. The most precious statues have vanished (only when religious belief is strong is the gold of the gods respected!). In 1939, however, under the paving of the Sacred Way, the remains were discovered of three large statues of wood or marble overlaid with gold and ivory, representing the Apollonian triad: Leto and her two children, Apollo and Artemis. One outstanding masterpiece, the *Auriga* or *Charioteer*, has survived to bear witness to the sumptuous refinement of the triumphal

and solitary confrontation with eternity, an exhilaration both oppressive and joyous, the only witness an eagle hovering high in the sky above the ruins, as if this were his personal domain.

The visitor should now take the Sacred Way which, turning sharply, leads to the great Temple of Apollo. On each side of the Sacred Way stood the votive monuments and the treasuries containing the sacred offerings and statues by which the wealthiest cities of Hellas showed the god their gratitude and veneration but by which they also

sculptures that were dedicated to Apollo. This bronze of the early fifth century, its workshop of origin unknown, shows Greek art freed from the traditional frontal posture, but still essentially restrained. This fascinating statue formed part of a large bronze *quadriga* (four-horse chariot) and might possibly have been accompanied by a figure of Polyzalus, tyrant of Gela in Sicily, the owner of the victorious chariot and the donor of the monument.

After this first impromptu visit to the museum (to which we shall return shortly), continuing along the Sacred Way you will come to the foundation wall of the sixth century Temple of Apollo; 117 metres long, the wall is an impressive sight and presents an astounding combination of the monumental and the refined in its construction of irregular limestone blocks chiselled smooth and perfectly assembled. Some guides will talk of a 'masterpiece of bonded masonry with curved joints', but these irritating and incomprehensive phrases betray a pretentious desire to impart information without caring if anyone understands.

The five erect columns of the majestic ruins of the Temple of Apollo belong to the fourth century temple which replaced a sixth century temple destroyed by an earthquake and built at the initiative of one of the most celebrated aristocratic families of Athens, the Alcmaeonidae, to which Clisthenes and Pericles and Alcibiades belonged through their mother. This famous temple had been constructed by means of subscriptions from all over Hellas and even beyond, for the Pharaoh of Egypt had made a generous contribution. It had been built on the site of an even earlier temple, probably dating from the beginning of the seventh century BC and destroyed by fire. But ancient monuments are rather like those Russian dolls which always contain another inside, and one must stop somewhere.

From the Temple of Apollo you can reach the theatre, which overlooks it; built in the fourth century BC and modified in the Roman period, the theatre has for the past two thousand years offered the visitor not the tragedies of Aeschylus and Sophocles, but one of the finest spectacles in the world – Delphi. Climbing up to the stadium, you discover another thrilling sight. The limestone tiers of the stadium date from the prodigality of Herod Atticus (second century AD); in the Classical period the Greeks sat on the beaten earth and left the stone for the gods.

In one of the rooms of the museum, which you should see both before and after visiting the site, are exhibited some of the champions who distinguished themselves in the stadium. The wrestler Agias and the runner Agelaus defy the passage of time in excellent copies of the originals of Lysippus. As one looks at these nudes, one realizes how deeply the Greeks loved the human body. The admirable backs reveal quite openly the physical attraction which the artist felt for beauty, strength and youth. Nowadays one smiles – such things have assumed a rather different aspect – and one forgets the virile nature of most of these friendships, the appeal which a mature man, the *eromenos*, could have for an adolescent, the *erastes*, who admired and listened to him. As girls rarely left the house and had no education, emotional adventure easily took another direction.

Delphi is the graveyard of Greece, a glorious and tragic graveyard. Here the Greek ideal of beauty was realized in gold, bronze, marble and stone; here also the ideal of the Greek mind found expression, an ethical system of moderation and harmony epitomized in wise maxims inscribed at the entrance to the temple: 'Nothing in excess', 'Learn to know yourself', 'Observe moderation and reason'. In speaking of man, the priests of Apollo could well have said, like Buddha: 'The string of the bow must be neither too loose nor too tight.' But at Delphi the Greeks also triumphantly engraved in stone their crimes against Hellas. Plutarch, who was a priest of the temple during the second century AD when Hadrian, Herod Atticus and the Antonines strove to restore the splendour of Delphi, was stirred to indignation when he read on the walls of the treasuries such shameful inscriptions as 'The Acanthians with the booty of the Athenians', 'The Athenians with the booty of the Corinthians' and 'The Phocians with the booty of the Thessalians'. Tragically, these monuments to the glory of the god of peace and concord were the fruit of the massacres, wars and plunderings by which ancient Greece was to destroy herself.

Leaving these mountains which bear witness to forces both divine and earthly, and to the greatness and the weakness of man, you go through the village of Delphi hidden discreetly behind a ridge and which today with its many hotels and shops has the clean and luxurious appearance of a Swiss mountain resort. Then you cross the plain of Amphissa covered with masses of olive-trees and go down to the sun and the sea of Itea. From this little port one can take a boat across to the peninsula of the Peloponnesus (now called Morea), attached to the extremity of Greece like a mis-shapen glove, where the different Hellenic peoples finally became intermingled – a wild land of legends and ruins that tell the whole story of Greece: Mycenae, Sparta, the Byzantine, Frankish, Venetian and Turkish occupations, and, finally, independence.

In Elis, a small, isolated and peaceful province of the Peloponnesus, twenty kilometres from the sea, lies one of the most famous places of the Hellenic world, **Olympia.** Not far from the Alphaeus, a river with a broad bed of pebbles and sand, shaded by pines and cypresses in gently undulating countryside, and bathed in a clear light, the ruins of Olympia blend with nature.

After the dramatic power of Delphi, the dreamy atmosphere of Olympia invites the visitor to saunter at leisure. Yet two thousand years ago, for a period of seven days every four years, this was the scene of the noisiest and most enthusiastic gathering in the whole of Greece. Our guide Pausanias, now assuming the function of a sports reporter, enables the visitor to relive the great moments of this sanctuary, and also to listen in to the gossip of the changing-room. But first of all one should read his account of the mythological origins of Olympia. The beautiful embroidered fabrics of legend always have a certain element of history as their basis. It seems that here too before the arrival of the Indo-European Hellenes, in the time of the Pelasgians (a legendary people of uncertain origin) the worship of the mother-goddess Gaea was practised, a cult with which her daughter Themis and her son Cronus must also have been associated; Cronus resided on the hill overlooking Olympia which was named after him, Cronion. On the arrival of the Achaeans, Zeus, regarded as the son of Cronus, succeeded him and established himself in the wood at the foot of Mount Cronion where an altar was erected in a clearing; later, the sacred wood or Altis was enclosed by a wall and decorated with *ex-voto* offerings; the first Temple of Hera was then built, in wood and stone, some time before the seventh century BC, and a round tumulus dedicated to Pelops was built in the open air (when Pausanias visited Olympia the mound was still being used for the sacrifice of black rams). Pelops, the first hero of Olympia, who had come with the invaders and was probably responsible for establishing the cult of Hera, wife of Zeus, has a history worth recounting.

Oenomaus, king of Pisa, a neighbouring city of which Olympia was a dependency until the beginning of the sixth century, had a sweet and pretty daughter, Hippodamia. Having learnt from an oracle that he would die on the day of her marriage, he eliminated all her suitors by challenging them to a chariot race which he always won with the winged horses lent by his father, the god Ares. Pelops then appeared, bribed the king's charioteer and arranged that the axle of the chariot should break during the race. The king, dragged along by his horses, perished, whereupon Pelops married the young virgin, became king and had numerous children. This story illustrates a Greek moral, the use of cunning and guile: Pelops and Ulysses are kindred spirits. The cult of Hercules, like that of Apollo, must have been introduced a little later, probably by the

Dorians; after cleaning out the stables of Augeas, Hercules founded the Olympic Games and, matching himself against his four brothers, became their first victor. After the Achaean and Dorian conquests, the Aetolians gave Elis and Olympia a period of stability. One of their number, Iphitus, appears to mark the beginning of the historic era; he negotiated the Sacred Truce by which the Olympic Games, at first local, then regional, eventually drew participants from the whole of Greece, becoming the great sporting and religious centre of the ancient world. The year 776 BC inaugurates the official era of the Olympiads (the four-year intervals between celebrations of the games) which soon served as the basis of Hellenic chronology.

The sixth century BC saw the construction of a new Heraion or Temple of Hera, an Archaic Doric edifice of which some of the peripteral columns were of wood. The stone enclosure of the Altis dates from the same period; from 470 to 457 BC the Temple of Zeus was built in its centre. Some twenty years earlier than the Parthenon, this temple was the most imposing religious structure of the sanctuary. Its raised base is of striking volume; in the grass beside it, leaning one against another, lie the enormous slices of stone that formed the drums of its columns. The temple contained a chryselephantine statue (i.e. marble overlaid with gold and ivory and set with precious stones), twelve to thirteen metres high, representing Zeus with a Victory in one hand and a sceptre surmounted by an eagle in the other. Counted as one of

the Seven Wonders of the World, the statue was the masterpiece of Phidias, who fashioned it in a neighbouring workshop that was converted into a church in Byzantine times. Through the centuries a succession of buildings appeared: the Prytaneion, serving as a refectory for public guests during the Olympic Games; the Theokoleon, where the high priests were accommodated; in the third century the Palaistra, with slender and exquisitely graceful columns; the Leonidaion, a hostelry named after its Naxian architect which was one of the largest buildings at Olympia; the Philippeion, erected in honour of Philip II of Macedon at the time of his victory; and finally the Roman constructions, the gymnasium, the baths and the vaulted entrance to the stadium (the length of the stadium, 192 metres, is supposed to have been measured out by a hundred paces of Hercules – the hero appears to have varied the length of his magnificent strides, for the stadium at Delphi measures 177 metres and that of Pergamum 210). The hippodrome or race course, dedicated to Pelops and to his victorious chariot, has vanished, swept away by the waters of the Alphaeus during one of this fickle river's changes of bed. All the edifices mentioned above now lie scattered in ruins among the grass and flowers, only a few rows of columns still standing here and there. The ruins bear witness to the deference shown by the German archaeologists who, after unearthing them during their excavations of 1875–1881, left them to mingle freely with nature, thus giving Olympia a profound charm of its own. The fact that the Altis or sacred wood, now covered with pines, formerly consisted of olives and plane-trees does not detract from the rustic appeal of this hallowed spot.

Olympia was at first under the domination of two neighbouring cities, Elis and Pisa; the former supplanted the latter at the beginning of the sixth century BC. The Elians administered the sanctuary from then onwards, trying to remain aloof from the great quarrels of the Greek world and cunningly seeking the protection of the dominant power: for a long time Sparta and then, when the time came, Philip II of Macedon. Finally, attentive as always to the political situation, Olympia gave the Romans a warm welcome even before they had begun their brutal conquest of Greece, thereby acquiring more or less enlightened protectors. Olympia was to witness the eccentricities of Nero; arriving there during the summer of AD 67, the emperor decided to bring forward the opening date of the games by three years, introduced a new competition for singing and music and, not content with winning this, had all the other prizes awarded to himself, even that of the chariot race in which he had fallen from his own *quadriga* (the Roman four-horse chariot). The emperor Hadrian attempted to revive the prestige of Olympia; he had a passion for Greece (his enemies called him 'Graeculus'), a passion which was to be embodied in the person of the charming Antinous. The sanctuary also benefited from the prodigality of the rhetorician Herod Atticus, who had given Athens its Odeon and Delphi its stone stadium; he provided Olympia with an aqueduct which, by diverting a tributary of the Alphaeus, brought Olympia the water and the freshness which it had always lacked in summer. The decline of Olympia, however, had begun as early as the second century BC, becoming more rapid in the second to fourth centuries AD. In AD 393 the Christian emperor Theodosius the Great prohibited the celebration of its pagan rites and had the statue of Zeus transported to Constantinople; the statue was destroyed shortly afterwards in a fire. The sanctuary itself was burned down by his successor, Theodosius II, in AD 426.

The Olympic charter which had established the Sacred Truce among all the Greek states made the city of Zeus the concrete symbol of Hellenic unity. The games, the celebration of which was assured by the soothsayers and the poets, had a deeply religious character which was preserved until the arrival of the Romans – their sacred origins were obvious, for had not the gods and heroes of mythology been the first champions? The Olympic festival officially lasted five days, the first and last days being set aside for worship and for thanksgiving to the gods. There were over eighty altars to be honoured. The first religious act marking the opening of the games seems to have been the sacrifice to Zeus Myodes ('Zeus the banisher of flies'). In his *Natural History* Pliny, who attended this ceremony in the Roman period, expresses his astonishment at its effectiveness: 'There is no animal less docile and less intelligent than the fly; the miracle of Olympia is all the more to be admired. [...] After the sacrifice of a bull to Zeus Myodes, the swarms of flies quietly leave the sacred ground.' Miracles abounded at this festival and the priests proved themselves adept in

conjuring tricks. The gullible Pausanias was amazed to see three empty bottles placed in the Temple of Dionysus and, after the doors had been closed and the locks sealed, to find them full the following day.

Throughout the duration of the festival the territory of Olympia was prohibited to married women; girls could enter the Altis or sacred grove, but according to Pausanias the only woman allowed to attend the games was the priestess of Demeter Chamyne. For a week at the end of June or in early July, Olympia became one vast fairground invaded by a motley crowd of 20,000 to 30,000 pilgrims who came from every part of Hellas, by boat, by chariot, on horseback or even on foot like Socrates. Tents appeared everywhere; persons of distinction enjoyed the privilege of living in the Altis; itinerant vendors sold honey-cakes and other refreshments, and also grains of incense and thanksgiving offerings for Zeus, Hera and Apollo. The intellectual and political élite of Greece gathered here: Pythagoras, Themistocles, Socrates, Plato and Demosthenes all came to Olympia. There were musicians, storytellers, acrobats, mountebanks and thieves. In this fantastic atmosphere both the noblest and the commonest distractions were available. The prohibition of married women and the presence of young girls made certain liberties possible during the hours of leisure. The Greeks would not have understood our false modesty, or, for that matter, our false boldness in such matters. Their sexual relationships were simple and natural, and even their notorious pederasty, an essentially military habit, was the manifestation not of truly abnormal complexes or inclinations but of vitality and a deep capacity for love – a handsome youth could arouse a stronger emotion than a girl. In any case in their eyes sex had no moral aspect. They revelled in the amorous adventures of Zeus and in the vagaries of Dionysus because these gods, made

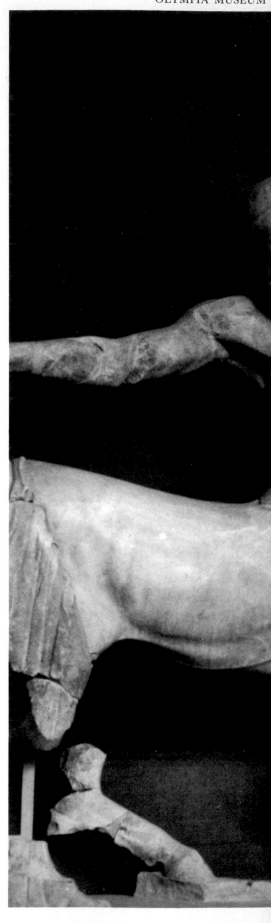

in their own image, reflected their own instincts. There was undoubtedly a much healthier quality and a greater erotic power in the enormous crudities of Aristophanes' comedies than is to be found in the vapid and miserable pornography of today.

The athletes trained at Olympia for nine months to prepare themselves for the three main days of the games. To compete they had to prove their status as Hellenes and freemen and to promise to respect the Olympic rules (*zanes*). Judging by the treasuries built by the cities of Cyrene, Sybaris, Byzantium, Selinus, Metapontium and Gela, competitors came from Sicily, Italy, Egypt, Cyrenaica and Asia Minor as early as the beginning of the fifth century BC. The morning of the first day was traditionally reserved for the three running races in the stadium, the most ancient of the contests: racing a single length of the stadium, racing double its length and racing under arms (that is, carrying one of the shields from the Temple of Zeus). The athletes ran naked, their bodies smeared with oil; they competed in fours and the winners took part in the final. The afternoon was devoted to the three forms of wrestling: straightforward wrestling using only the flat of the hand; a very violent kind of boxing (the combatants, their fists fastened with leather thongs provided with metal knobs, often emerged from the contest bruised and bleeding, and some were even killed); and the *pancration* or all-in wrestling, in which any kind of blow was permissible and which was rather similar to our modern 'catch' wrestling.

On the second day the horse-races were held. Horse and rider had to circle the track of the racecourse (*hippodromos*) twelve times, covering about 4,500 metres. There were also contests for four-horse and two-horse chariots, and, at a later stage, races with chariots drawn by colts, mares and mules.

The third day of the games was

reserved for the *pentathlon*, the competition in which victory carried the highest honours. The contestants had to take part in five successive events: jumping, throwing the discus, throwing the javelin, the single-length sprint and wrestling. For the jumping contest the participants stood on a mound, obtaining their momentum by swinging their arms with a dumb-bell in each hand, and were thus able to leap a distance of up to fifty feet. The discus, which had a hole in the centre, was much heavier than its modern counterpart. The javelin, thrown with the aid of a leather thong, had to hit a target. The first three events were eliminating contests; the winners competed against each other in the sprint, and the best of these faced each other in the wrestling event.

On the last day of the Olympic Games the ceremonial distribution of laurel-wreaths took place. Sacrifices were offered to the gods and great banquets were held as the victors, their families and their cities rejoiced in their success. The prize received by the triumphant athlete was a simple wreath of olive-branches, cut with a golden scythe from the sacred tree of Olympia. He had fought for glory, to assert the supremacy of his city in physical strength and skill. This has sometimes been interpreted as the sign of an aristocratic ideology which gave priority to the best, exalting the individual, an ideology that has been contrasted with the egalitarian ideal of Athenian democracy. But it must be remembered that Athenian democracy had been the idea of aristocrats, such as Clisthenes and Pericles, and that, when individual virtue disappeared, democracy was to become demagogy. It must also be stressed that the feats of the Olympic athlete were a collective experience closely linked with the honour of his family and of his city. After his coronation, the champion was lauded by the poets; Pindar specialized in such verse and in his first *Olympics* sang the praises of Hieron of Syracuse and Theron of Agrigentum, two tyrants who took a pride in owning successful stables. The champion was also carved in stone by the great sculptors: Phidias, Polycletus – whose *Doryphorus* (javelin-thrower) became one of the chief models of ancient sculpture – and Myron, whose *Discobolus* (discus-thrower) survives in Roman copies, all worked at Olympia, as did Praxiteles and Lysippus in later times.

Yet, even in the intoxication of victory (fathers readily died of joy at such moments, according to the ancient chronicles), it was necessary to observe moderation in keeping with Greek morality. Between two lyrical flights of fancy Pindar gives this warning: 'If someone attains the summit of happiness, let him be content to enjoy it and not attempt to raise himself to the level of the gods.' It was said that the celebrated Milo of Crotona (not Croto of Milona, as some learned sports writer has recently said!), six times victor in the wrestling contest, died

because of his overweening confidence with his hands trapped in a split in an oak-tree, the tree of Zeus, which he had wanted to break by his own strength – a cruel way of being 'rapped on the knuckles by the gods', as Aristophanes would have said. In his halcyon days the same Milo of Crotona, according to Pausanias, used to walk through the Altis with a calf on his shoulders, which he later killed and then ate.

The Olympic Games had their critics. Xenophanes, a

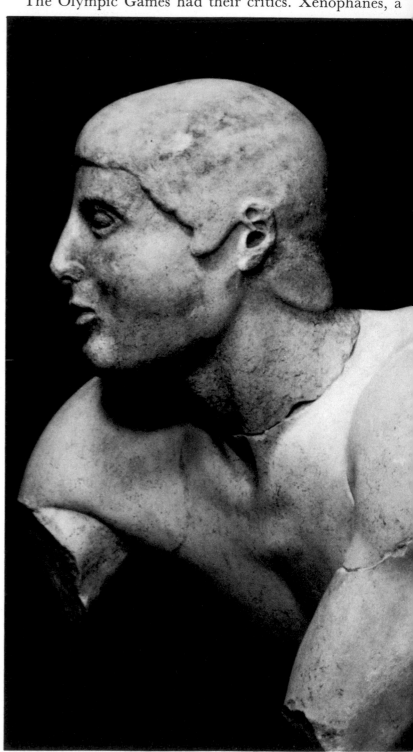

famous bard of the sixth century BC who used to travel from city to city reciting his poems, wrote indignantly: 'It is not right to set strength above wisdom; a city will not be better governed simply because one of its children has won the prize for boxing, wrestling, the pentathlon or the foot-race' – a pertinent observation, even if it suggests a rather narrow intellectual severity. Socrates and Plato both thought that beauty and virtue were identical, that a beautiful body was only the reflection of a beautiful soul, which is not as absurd as one might imagine: physical strength and harmony are not merely a gift, but are often acquired by self-discipline, effort and reason, especially when, as in the Greek ethic, there is a clearly fixed human ideal – *kallos kagathos*, 'beautiful and good'. To be fortunate in one's bodily endowments gives a person a stability and a physical security which are reflected in behaviour and which breed simplicity, generosity and also courage – the very qualities which the Greeks regarded as the principal

virtues. Modern man, marked by Christian civilization which has attributed a sense of merit to anxiety and suffering, and which has separated the mind and the body, emphasizing the inferiority of the latter, has difficulty in understanding the importance that the Greeks attached to the body, the equality of status which it shared with its partner, the mind. But, since the marriage of mind and body is the great mystery and adventure of the human condition, were not the Greeks right to honour it so gloriously?

There is an interesting text by Epictetus in which he attempts to discourage a youth intent on becoming an Olympic champion. Epictetus enumerates all the privations and sufferings that he will have to endure, the efforts that he will have to make; he talks of the dust that he will have to swallow, the heat that he will have to bear, the blows and injuries that he will inevitably receive; he brandishes the spectre of defeat, encountered much more often than victory, and concludes suddenly: 'And if, after that, you are still keen, then go ahead!' Here is the essence of the Greek ethic: prudence and moderation, but also joy and spontaneity in action.

Olympia played a cultural role of great importance in ancient Greece. It was here that Herodotus achieved fame by reading his *History of the Persian Wars*; it was here, too, that Isocrates declaimed in 380 BC his celebrated *Panegyric,* a hymn to the glory of Greece in which he attempted to convince Athens that its historic mission was to unite the Greeks of Europe peacefully in order to free the Greeks of Asia from the Persian yoke; with a lucidity that unfortunately proved ineffective he declared: 'The name of Hellene is not only that of a race, it is above all that of a civilization.'

There were three other great centres where Pan-Hellenic games were held: Corinth, Nemea and Delphi; but none of these attained the renown of Olympia, where Zeus himself crowned those who displayed in high degree the physical and moral qualities appropriate to man, the qualities that formed what the Greeks called *aretē,* a word difficult to translate but which in fact expresses Nietzsche's idea of a nucleus of vital energy.

The **Museum at Olympia** is exceptionally interesting and has a large number of exhibits. The principal sculptures found by the German archaeologists during their excavations are still displayed in the old museum, a modest but unpretentious building; they are shortly to be transferred to the new museum, which is certainly much more functional, though its rather unattractive modern architecture may seem a little incongruous in this setting. The decorative elements of the two pediments of the Temple of Zeus are exhibited in their original arrangement, the most significant sculptural ensemble in the whole of Greece and one of the finest achievements of Greek statuary. This is an art that had just emerged from Archaism and was entering its Classical period; if it does not yet possess the freedom and suppleness that Phidias and his pupils were to show twenty-five years later at the Acropolis, it nevertheless has a wonderful power and breadth. The west pediment is a masterpiece, allegedly depicting the battle between the Lapithae and the Centaurs at the marriage-feast of Pirithous. This traditional interpretation, however, is disputed: the Lapithae were a people of Thessaly and it is difficult to see why the priests of Olympia should have chosen such a geographically remote legend; and the Centaurs, half men and half horses who lived in the woods and whose lewd appetites were always stimulated by drinking, had certainly conducted their exploits in lands far from Olympia. The group of statues, despite important gaps, suggests a powerful impression of movement and action: one of the Centaurs is seen crushing a woman's breast, another savagely biting a young man's arm, and various fragments convey the violence of abduction, the impatience of rape. Apollo appears above the tumult, supreme and indifferent, his arm held out in a pacifying gesture; the same absence of feeling is discernible on the faces of the women being raped. In the Classical period the Greeks, though a vehement and passionate people, endowed serenity with the attributes of nobility and dignity; smooth, unchanging faces symbolized beauty, grace and virtue. In contrast, one observes the grimacing countenances of the Centaurs, the indication of an expressionism that was to become increasingly common from the fourth century BC, culminating in the art of Pergamum in the second century BC; the altar of Zeus (now in the East Berlin museum) is the most striking example of this extravagance, both in feeling and in sheer size, which became characteristic of the Hellenistic art that bears the imprint of Alexander's ambitions and of Asiatic influences.

Twelve metopes representing the labours of Hercules decorated the frieze running round the peristyle of the Temple of Zeus; three of the best preserved, removed by a team of French archaeologists who visited Morea in 1829, are now in the Louvre in Paris; the other nine are badly damaged – one of the more complete metopes shows Hercules supporting the world, aided by the goddess Athena, while Atlas offers him the golden apples from the garden of the Hesperides; the impassive faces again reveal the contempt for emotion typical of the Greek artists of the Classical age. The Archaic smile, that wonderful token of complicity, had gone for ever; when sensation and feeling reappeared in Greek art, they were often merely the expression of a facile self-indulgence.

One of the statues in the museum,

the *Hermes Dionysophorus* ('Hermes carrying Dionysus'), discovered in the *naos* or inner sanctuary of the Heraion, is world-famous and has been excessively commercialized by souvenir statuettes. The experts cannot agree if this is an original work by Praxiteles that has been miraculously preserved, or a Hellenistic or even a Roman copy. It is difficult to know if a particular work was in fact carved by a great sculptor when one has no reliable point of reference by which to establish a comparison (the Greek copyists working for Rome had a perfect technique). However, certainty in such matters usually seems to be prompted at least partly by emotion, and so a diagnosis becomes a question of feeling and instinct as much as of knowledge; the author's personal conviction is that this is a copy, albeit an excellent one, in which something is missing – not so much the hand of the artist as his spirit. At all events, the *Hermes* does not possess the freedom and the sensuality which permeate the Roman copy of the *Aphrodite of Cnidus* now in the Louvre. It is true, moreover, that Praxiteles, well-known for his liaison with the beautiful courtesan Phryne, was a *genre* artist with a gift for satisfying the taste for elegance characteristic of his times (mid-fourth century BC). The *Hermes* of Olympia and the *Aphrodite* of Arles are both perfect works in which the lack of vigour and emotion is not necessarily the fault of copyists. The *Hermes Dionysophorus* has, however, an admirable back, and on the religious level it is an important statue, showing the messenger of Zeus taking the infant Dionysus, born of the loves of Zeus and Semele, far from the wrath of Hera. The child Dionysus, a reincarnation of a long-familiar divinity, represents a new hope, the promise of a future life and of a better world; the fervent cult of Dionysus was to rekindle Greek religion in the fourth century BC and, to a certain extent, it prepared people's minds for the birth

of Christianity. In the kindness of Hermes for the child whom he holds on one arm and amuses with a bunch of grapes, there is almost a foreshadowing of another protector of travellers, St Christopher carrying the Child Jesus.

Leaving Olympia and passing through Langada, Dimitsana and Kårytaina, picturesque mountain villages lying below Frankish ruins, you cross Arcadia on the way to Tripolis, where the road to Sparta and Mistra begins. Arcadia, a wild and isolated region covered with pine-forests and dominated by the snow-capped peaks of Mount Lycaeus and Mount Taygetus, is probably richer in legend and mythology than any other part of Greece. The Arcadians claimed to be the first inhabitants of the Peloponnesus; in fact, they were of Achaean origin and had been protected from the Dorian invasion by the impregnability of their territory, which served as a natural fortress.

On Mount Lycaeus, Zeus was supposed to have fallen in love with the nymph Callisto, the companion of Artemis. Two boys were born of their love: Arcas, whom the jealous Hera immediately changed into a bear-cub, and Pan, bearded, horned and with a cleft foot, half man and half goat, and of a highly lascivious nature. Arcas gave his name to the country, while Pan became the protecting household god, the invisible friend of shepherds and hunters.

The Arcadians, a wild, primitive people, showed a more tender disposition only in music. Hermes, born in this country, was supposed to have fashioned the first lyre with the shell of a tortoise and the bowels of a lamb; the ingenious Pan, for his part, transformed a nymph into reeds which he then assembled to make his famous pipes. It was no doubt because of this musical past that the rugged and austere Arcadia became, under the writer's pen and the artist's brush, the ideal country, the mythical kingdom of the idyll, the ecloguc and the pastoral poem, and that its praises were sung by Horace, Ronsard and André de Chénier, who visited it only in their imagination.

By making a brief detour through Andritsaina and taking a new road running above the valley of the Alphaeus, you will come to the **Temple of Bassae,** surrounded by the highest mountain peaks in the Peloponnesus. The temple's isolated situation has saved it from being plundered for building materials, and it is in a remarkable state of preservation. It was discovered in 1764 by the French architect Bocher; unfortunately, in 1812 two Englishmen, Cokerell and Forster, trying to emulate Lord Elgin, organized an expedition and removed the sculptures of its frieze – twenty-three bas-reliefs that were sold shortly afterwards to the Regent (later George IV) and placed in the British Museum, where they remain to this day.

According to Pausanias, the temple of Bassae was erected in this sublime setting by the inhabitants of Phigalia in thanksgiving to Apollo for having protected their city during an epidemic of plague; they appear to have employed the services of Ictinus, the architect of the Parthenon. The temple, with its peristyle of thirty-eight

THE TEMPLE OF BASSAE

slender Doric columns, combines grace and austerity; it is smaller than the Parthenon (38 × 14 metres compared with 69 × 30) and was built twenty years later, in the rough and dark local limestone, which in the setting sun is bathed in pink and lilac tints. Its interior structure is highly original: five Ionic columns are imbedded in the side-walls of the *naos* or sanctuary, at the end of which stands the first Corinthian column ever discovered. In its wild and awesome setting the temple of Bassae is equalled only by that of Segesta in Sicily; its isolated situation and severe beauty are deeply moving.

The road from Tripolis to **Sparta** crosses a barrier of mountains and comes out into the valley of the Eurotas, one of the few rivers in Greece where water flows all the year round. Enclosed by the snow-capped peaks of Mount Parnon to the east and Mount Taygetus to the west, where Homer sets his description of the adventures of Artemis, the 'goddess with the bow', and her companions, this plain presents an unexpected luxuriance quite unlike the kind of scenery that one would associate with the austerity and rigour of Sparta. Yet this little paradise of orchards and meadows is the very heart of Laconia and the cradle of Sparta, also called Lacedaemon (an older name probably dating from the Mycenaean age and which referred to the whole region). The delightful patchwork of orange-, lemon- and mulberry-trees which you see today did not have quite this splendour in ancient times, but the rich and well-watered land was suitable for stockraising and for cultivating corn, vines and olive-trees. Jean-Louis Vaudoyer, who has written so lovingly of Greece, was astonished to discover the little island of Platanistas, thickly wooded with trees of delicate foliage, where, under the shade of poplars and willows, one could drink a cup of coffee and listen to the cooing of turtle-doves. It was here that young Spartans played their violent games, where naked girls and boys fought ferociously, trying to throw their adversaries into the river, and where, in an enclosure dedicated to Artemis, children were whipped until they bled so that they would learn not to cry out but to overcome suffering. The French historian Taine, who presented man as a chameleon always reflecting the colours of his environment, was not infallible; a rustic background may well have been at the origin of the poetic genius of Virgil and La Fontaine, but it also helped to form the best soldiers of Antiquity; appropriately, this green, joyous plain is enclosed by a rampart-wall of mountains that extends as far as the sea.

Modern Sparta, built shortly after Greece won her independence, under the reign of her first king, Otto of Bavaria (1832–61), is a characterless town with hardly a trace of its glorious past. The museum contains only a few *ex-voto* objects, for the excavations of the British School proved disappointing. This is the result not of the vicissitudes of history, but of the determination of the Lacedaemonians, a people hostile to wealth and luxury, not to build any expensive monuments and to erect only modest temples to the gods. Sparta prided itself in being a powerful military encampment, not a city bedecked with ornaments and works of art. Thucydides was thus able to anticipate the disappointment felt by the visitor of today: 'If Sparta were to be laid waste and if there remained only the foundations of its sanctuaries and public buildings, posterity would find it difficult to believe that this city was powerful enough to justify its reputation.' In Greece, ruins usually stimulate the imagination, but at Sparta the imagination has nothing on which to feed, except for the writing-tablets of history and the accounts of Thucydides, Xenophon, Plato and Plutarch who was its champion in the Roman period.

Laconia appears to have played an important role as early as the Mycenaean age; around the tenth century BC it was conquered by the Dorian invaders, who founded Sparta, the name of the city doubtless deriving from the broom (*spartos*) which grew in abundance on the plain. In the eighth century the Spartans crossed the Taygetus and took possession of Messenia with its fertile plain; but in the following century the Messenians revolted and they were finally suppressed only after a fierce struggle lasting some thirty years. By this time the social, political and military structure of Sparta had been firmly established, and it was to remain unchanged for nearly 500 years. The introduction of the laws by which the city was ruled was attributed to Lycurgus, probably a mythical figure. In fact, rather similar customs and practices have been observed in the primitive societies of Africa and Oceania. This rigidity, the blind submission to rules of ancient origin, was in marked contrast with the evolution of the other Greek cities, which looked on Sparta with a mixture of astonishment and fear.

The population was divided into three classes: the free citizens, the 'equals', appear never to have exceeded 11–12,000; the slaves or helots were ten times more numerous (their origins probably date from the Dorian conquest and the subjugation of the old Achaean population, though this view is disputed); the *perioikoi*, whose status was rather similar to that of the metics in Athens, but whose influence was much less, were mainly farmers, occupying the borderland between Laconia and Messenia. The rich plains of the Eurotas and the Pamisus belonged to the city-state and were distributed in equal lots (*kleroi*) to the citizens; these lands were cultivated by the helots, who were serfs without rights or protection, and the revenue from them was collected by the citizens or 'equals'. This class of military citizens devoted all their time to the service and defence of the city, beginning their apprenticeship in childhood. At the age of seven the child left his family; he learnt to count and read, and was taught music, but already instructors were preparing him for the rigorous life of the warrior, disciplining his body and hardening his heart with rhythmic exercizes and violent contests. Plutarch relates the story of the Spartan child who hid a fox-cub under his cloak and allowed it to tear his flesh, without a murmur of complaint, rather than admit to theft. Military service proper was performed from the ages of sixteen to twenty, during which time the Spartan youth began to form those special friendships which, far from weakening the warrior virtues, developed into a virile comradeship with his elders, who were stronger and more battle-hardened. Before becoming a fully-fledged *hoplite*, he had to undergo the final test of the *krypteia*, a tradition of a rather mysterious nature: it seems that the young man (*eirēn*) went out into a wild part of the country, where he lived like a wolf-man; then he would set out on a manhunt, which ended in the putting to death of a helot. Between the ages of twenty and thirty the young Spartan, even if he was married, lived a communal life with his fellow-soldiers and slept under canvas; only later did he dwell in the house for which his wife was responsible, and he still attended the communal meals (*syssitia*), which bore no resemblance to the merry banquets of the Athenians: the sole fare provided was a broth of black flour, the symbol of Spartan austerity. Their red tunics, on which the blood of wounds blended with the colour of the cloth, and their long hair distinguished the hoplites of Sparta from those of other cities. They could manoeuvre with a rapidity and a discipline which excited the admiration of Xenophon, changing from marching formation to battle order in an instant. When the Greeks rose up against the invader in the Persian wars, there was no question of denying Sparta supreme command.

Whereas in Athens girls rarely left the house until they were married – a tradition which, outside the large cities, has survived in Greece to the present day – in Sparta they led a boy's life: they would wrestle with each other and throw the discus and javelin, so that they would be able to give the city fine, strong children. A great freedom of behaviour appears to have been customary; Spartan girls were often naked when they danced and sang at public festivities and ceremonies; even when married they continued to make love with other men. According to Plutarch, a Spartan man who fancied the wife of a comrade would inform the husband of his desires and usually received permission to satisfy them. It was thus official practice for children to be conceived in other men's beds. Such habits amazed the other Greek cities, which were certainly not prudish.

The political organization of Sparta, like its social

structure, was primitive. The 'equals' or free citizens formed an assembly of the people with limited powers. Sparta was the only Greek city to remain faithful to monarchy: two hereditary kings belonging to two unrelated families shared an authority closely resembling that of the Homeric kings; they were both religious and military leaders. In times of peace the real power was exercised by five magistrates, the *ephoroi*, and a council of thirty members, the *gerousia*. This was an oligarchy founded on an extremely narrow base. Yet the machinery proved effective for a long period. In the sixth century BC Sparta had compelled all the cities of the peninsula, except Argos and Achaia, to join the Peloponnesian League. After their common victory over the Persians (481), Sparta allowed Athens to reap all the material benefits. An austere, aloof city, it was chiefly concerned to see that its laws were enforced; it fought only to secure its authority over the neighbouring cities. The expansionist colonial ambitions of Pericles and Alcibiades were foreign to it; when the time came, it was to oppose those ambitions, making itself the champion of Greek liberties. Only with its victory over Athens after a war lasting thirty years did Sparta lay claim to hegemony; even then, its imperialism was directed mainly against the cities of Asia Minor and its former ally, the king of Persia. The annihilation of the Lacedaemonian fleet at Cnidus by Conon, the general defeated at Aigospotami who had joined the Persian camp, was a cruel blow. The defeat of its supposedly invincible army at Leuctra (371), by the Boeotians and their Athenian allies, heralded the emergence of a new military supremacy, that of Thebes. Henceforth Sparta, in spite of heroic attempts at recovery, suffered a rapid decline, and soon the whirlwind of the Macedonian conquest was to engulf it along with the other cities of Greece.

It is easy to see some of the reasons for Sparta's decadence. First of all, its fierce determination to remain static prevented all progress (the success of Thebes was due partly to the tactical innovations of its generals, Pelopidas and Epaminondas). The main factor, however, was its social system: the élite, who shared all the best land among themselves, found that it was to their advantage to restrict the number of births, a policy that led to demographic disaster. In 479 BC, at Plataea, there had been 5,000 Spartan foot-soldiers; in 371 BC, at Leuctra, there were only 800. Moreover, after the capture of Athens which had brought the Peloponnesian War to a victorious conclusion, the Spartan troops of Lysander and King Agesilaus set about plundering the wealthy cities of Asia Minor – Aeolia, Phocaea and Lydia; the prodigious booty which they brought back to their city marked the beginning of an inequality of fortunes, an appetite for riches and for pleasures, which were contrary to the social ethic of Sparta and jeopardized the cohesion of the citizen class, the 'equals'.

The inhumanity of the fate of the helots, who were treated as mere cattle, has often been emphasized. It seems that the Spartans used the confrontation between the propertied class and the exploited class as an instrument for maintaining the city in a perpetual state of alert and compelling it to preserve its warrior virtues. The drunken helot who used to be shown to Spartan children to encourage sober habits is a significant illustration of the deterrent function of the slave in Sparta. The state of insecurity which the city deliberately sustained was to lead to bloody clashes and revolts, notably in 464 BC when, after an earthquake had destroyed Sparta, a large number of helots rose up in rebellion, marched on the city and were halted only with great difficulty. Sparta has often been regarded as the model of the Fascist state, its social structure being seen as proof of a racialist policy of extermination; nowadays the association of Fascism with ancient Sparta is no longer a commonplace, though it is still sometimes suggested by persons who like to put forward the idea merely to display their learning. The reality was more complex. It would be nearer the truth, and also more original, to see the caste of Spartan 'equals' as the ancestors of the Knights Templars and the Teutonic Knights. There certainly existed a Spartan morality which, though related to primitive and barbarous traditions, was not without courage and grandeur. In constructing his ideal republic, Plato adopted certain Spartan laws which he considered necessary for the physical and moral well-being of the city. Thucydides quotes a speech of the Spartan king Archidamus II which reveals a wisdom quite alien to totalitarian mythology: 'There is no great difference between one man and another [. . .] individual merit can be acquired if it is sought rigorously and with perseverance.'

Leaving this city which has become no more than an abstract idea, the traveller will find a thrilling visual experience awaiting him some five kilometres from Sparta, as **Mistra** comes into view. From a distance this Byzantine city of the fourteenth and fifteenth centuries, dominated by a thirteenth-century Frankish fortress, does not give the impression of being deserted. Jean-Louis Vaudoyer describes it as 'a great amphitheatre overgrown with hardy plants where, among the cypresses and the orange-trees, are the fabulous rounded domes of The Thousand and One Nights, in colours of turquoise, coral and jade'. Climbing its lanes is hard work and from close to it is all rather depressing, but among the chaos of ruined houses you will find a dozen or so chapels, churches and monasteries almost intact. The monasteries of the Peribleptos and Pantanassa – the 'Queen of the World' seated beside Christ Pantocrator, the omnipotent God of Byzantine theology – contain frescoes that possess a certain style, though dating from the late Byzantine period and in many cases badly restored. At Mistra the visitor will find no masterpieces but instead a

powerful aura of mystery. The history of this place provides a vivid contrast to that of Sparta.

The Fourth Crusade, diverted from its original purpose, ended in the sack of Constantinople (AD 1204) and the distribution of the Christian Empire of the East among the princes of the West. Greece formed part of the territory acquired by Venice and the Franks. The Peloponnesus, which now became the principality of Morea and Achaia, was the apanage of Geoffroy de Villehardouin, an all-powerful prince who struck his own coin and allotted fiefs to his dukes and great barons – La Trémoille, Toucy, Lusignan, Agout, Brienne and Périgord. The whole region was dotted with fortresses. Geoffroy's son, Guillaume de Villehardouin, built the fortress at Mistra in 1249; but, taken prisoner by the emperor Michael Palaeologus, he was forced to surrender it. The Byzantines, basing their campaign on this stronghold, raised the whole of Laconia in rebellion against the Franks; fifty years later, helped by the quarrels and rivalries that erupted among the Frankish barons, they had succeeded in driving them from nearly the entire peninsula. The 'New France', as Pope Honorius had called it, had not lasted a century. It is not possible here to recount the stirring adventure of the Frankish kingdoms of the Orient, an adventure that had begun with the founding of the kingdom of Jerusalem in 1099 and ended with the fall of the kingdom of Cyprus in 1571; or to describe the splendours of these feudal courts, of which the Norman kingdom of Sicily provided the most magnificent example. Goethe resuscitated Mistra and its Frankish knights by choosing it as the setting for the second part of *Faust*. But it was Byzantium that gave glory and prosperity to this city, which it built and occupied for nearly 200 years. Under the rule of the Cantacuzene and Palaeologus despots (the brothers or sons of the emperor of Byzantium, to whom Morea was traditionally awarded as an apanage), it numbered about 50,000 inhabitants, becoming the metropolis of the Peloponnesus and the cultural centre of Greece. If the vestiges of the palace of the despots betray an Italianate style, this is only poetic justice, for Mistra had given the Medici court its most illustrious philosopher, Gemiste Plethon. At the time of its greatest wealth, due largely to the breeding of the silkworm, and its most intense artistic activity, Mistra was struck by the Turkish invasion in 1460, seven years after the fall of Constantinople. Subjected to Venetian rule from 1687 to 1715, Mistra remained an active city, but during the second Turkish occupation it suffered an abrupt decline; in 1770 it was burnt down in an uprising of the Mainotes and was never to recover. The Mainotes, who inhabit the Maina, an impregnable natural fortress formed by the southern extremity of the Taygetus mountains, are a people apart, fierce warriors of wild and distinctly feudal customs. In their love of liberty they have always resisted the foreign occupants of their country, whether Roman, Frankish or Turkish; during the Greek War of Independence their 10,000 bandit-soldiers were to play a decisive role.

Mistra still has a few inhabitants – priests and nuns whose warm but dignified welcome has the grace characteristic of all Greeks. Perhaps, like the author, you will leave Mistra to the loud peals of a bell, as if the spirits of the past were saying goodbye.

If you have time to dally a little longer, you should visit the southern Peloponnesus and see Monemvasia (in the Middle Ages the name became Malvoisie, still famous as the name of the local wines), a pretty little town perched proudly on a rock with Venetian fortifications, a Byzantine church and ancient houses. You should also go to Mavromati, the ancient Messene, which after the defeat of Sparta at Leuctra was restored to independence by the Boeotians. Its walls, one of the finest examples of ancient fortification, were erected by one of the great men of Thebes, the general Epaminondas. The theatre, built against the mountainside, is of modest dimensions but graceful proportions and is set in a burning, melancholy countryside.

The traveller fond of historical memories can also go on to the port of Navarino, near the ancient Pylos, the homeland of the wise Nestor. Here, in June 1827, as the result of a misunderstanding, the allied fleet of twenty-seven British, French and Russian vessels and the Turco-Egyptian fleet of eighty-nine ships engaged battle, their guns blasting at close quarters. Most of the Turco-Egyptian ships were sunk, but the more solid structures of the Great Powers remained afloat. This Ottoman catastrophe, described by the Duke of Wellington as an 'untoward event', proved to be the first step towards the liberation of Greece.

Greek independence, foreshadowed by the victory of Navarino, was finally proclaimed two years later at **Nauplia,** at the other extremity of the Peloponnesus. Situated at the head of the gulf of Argos, this small town with its pretty roofs of round tiles, occupied by the Venetians from 1389 to 1540 and again from 1686 to 1715, still bears the mark of the republic of the Venetian doges. Wrested from the Turks by the patriots at the outset of the War of Independence, it was the capital of liberated Greece for five years (1829–34). Here, on 9 October 1831, Capodistria, the head of the first Hellene government, was assassinated; and on 5 February 1833 Nauplia witnessed the coronation of King Otto I, the Bavarian prince chosen by the allied powers to prevent the heroic young state from being plunged into anarchy. When Athens became the capital, Nauplia continued to be associated with the fortunes of Otto I; in 1862 the rebellion of its garrison gave the signal for the insurrection that resulted in his removal from the throne. A year later, Great Britain found a new king, George I, whose Danish dynasty was henceforth to share the tumultuous political destiny of Greece. Within a

hundred years the Greeks were to see six kings – George I assassinated, the pro-German Constantine overthrown (1917) and George II abdicating (1923), though both the last-named returned to the throne – several military *coups*, the ubiquitous influence of a politician, Venizelos (1909–34), twelve years of republican government (1924–36), the dictatorship of General Metaxas (1936–41), a heroic resistance to a cruel occupation during the Second World War, and then a disastrous and bloody civil war. As for the events of the present day, interpretations differ according to individual temperament: some side with Creon, others with little Antigone. How difficult men find it to strike a happy medium between the brutal rigidity of Sparta and the ruinous disorder of demagogy!

If Nauplia serves as a reminder of the modest origins of modern Greece, which at first comprised only 600,000 inhabitants occupying poor, mountainous land, its monument to the Philhellenes also bears witness to the spirit of enthusiasm and dedication to which this country owed its rebirth; the marble pyramid was erected to the memory of Marshal Maison, General Fabvier, Admiral de Rigny, and the French soldiers and sailors who died for Greek independence. As soon as the ambitions of Napoleon had been finally thwarted, the élites of Europe committed themselves with burning fervour to the Greek cause. London, Milan and Paris created committees to support the Society of Friends founded by Ypsilanti at Odessa in 1815. In 1824 Lord Byron, one of the most passionate champions of Greece, died at Missolonghi. If the game played by the Great Powers (Britain, France and Russia), anxious to respect the 'European order', often proved disappointing, the support given by thousands of generous hearts was to enable the Greek resistance, sustained by the mountain populations, the shipowners and the middle class, to assume a national dimension.

It is thought that Nauplia, whose name means 'naval station', was founded by Eastern navigators whom legend personified in the figure of Palamedes, the most cunning of Greeks according to Homer. Palamedes is supposed to have invented the games of dice, chess and cards to amuse the Achaeans during the siege of Troy, and is also accredited with the invention of lighthouses, the calendar and even the alphabet. Nauplia remained under Byzantine rule until 1210, when it was seized by the Franks; in 1377 the Franks were replaced by the Venetians, who succeeded in resisting the assaults of the Turks until 1540 – not as long as at Heraklion, but nevertheless for nearly a century after the conquest of Morea. In the fifteenth and sixteenth centuries, the Venetians built the citadel of Acronauplia, which occupies the entire peninsula, doubling the Frankish fortifications. During their second occupation of the town, at the end of the seventeenth and beginning of the eighteenth centuries, they erected the fortress that overlooks the town, from the plans drawn up by the French colonel, La Salle. The fortress is an imposing structure, approached by a flight of 857 steps (there is also a road which cars can take). The view is superb; from the fortress you can look out over the pretty roofs of Romanesque tiles and view the vast panorama of the gulf of Argos. Happy and carefree, Nauplia seems to turn its back on its hinterland, as if it wanted to know nothing of the monstrous crimes committed by the families of the Pelopidae and the Atridae in Archaic times, when kings and queens, guilty of parricide, fratricide and incest, killed and devoured each other at hideous banquets. Nauplia looks out to sea and into the setting sun, which presents some magnificent sights: touches of gold and vermilion on the waters of the gulf, and broad trails of orange, crimson or purple over the distant blue and grey mountains

of Parnon.

If you stay two or three days in Nauplia (the hotels are pleasant and comfortable – one of them, on the isle of Bourzi, occupies a small Venetian fortress) you will be able to visit Argos and Lerna, which you will have glimpsed on the way from Tripolis. Whether you go to these sites depends on your own particular fancies, for neither can claim to kindle strong emotions. Argos, inhabited from the second millennium BC, became one of the most powerful cities of the Peloponnesus at the time of the Dorian conquest. Its civilization was long and brilliant, and it boasted a famous school of bronze-workers which achieved renown in the works of Hageladas, at the end of the sixth century BC, and those of his pupil, Polycletus. But Argos was to suffer an abrupt decline. Today its ruins, dating mostly from Roman times, cannot match the greatness of its reputation. The museum contains some Archaic bronze armour and swords which are probably not very different from those worn by Diomedes, the king of Argos 'with the mighty war-cry' who came to Troy with eighty ships. The beauty of the women of Argos was extolled by Homer; one of them, Danae, was immortalized by the brushes of Titian and Tintoretto. The prisoner of her father Acrisius, a descendant of Danaüs (who had fled from Egypt with his fifty daughters), Danae was impregnated by Zeus in the form of a shower of gold which, in the paintings of the great masters, seems to have given her little pleasure. This rather peculiar union resulted in the birth of Perseus, the hero whose two most celebrated exploits were the rescue of Andromeda, an innocent girl who was the prisoner of a sea monster, and the slaying of Medusa, the Gorgon from whose blood was born the horse Pegasus and whose head appears as an emblem on the armour of Athena.

Lerna was one of the richest sources of myth in Argolis. Its three springs and its marsh were renowned. Hercules had to cut off the constantly reappearing heads of the Hydra which lived in the plague-ridden and bottomless waters of the marsh (this was one of the entrances to the underworld, used by Hades when he had ravished Persephone and also by Dionysus when he visited the shade of his mother, the mortal Semele). The ruins of Lerna, unearthed by the American School, will appear modest to the uninitiated, but they represent a rare example of Early Helladic architecture (2600–2000 BC). During this period preceding the Indo-European invasions Greece acquired populations who had come from Asia Minor and who, mingling with the inhabitants of the Neolithic period, gave form to a new civilization, that of the early Bronze Age.

From Nauplia you can reach **Epidaurus** by a road that winds in and out of a gentle countryside of fields, meadows and woods of pines and holm oaks, its undulations gradually diminishing towards the sea and the port of Troezene where the pilgrims disembarked in Antiquity. The creation of the sanctuary of Asclepius at Epidaurus and its success were undoubtedly the work of shrewd and enterprising priests, for according to tradition Asclepius was a native of Thessaly, in northern Greece. In the *Iliad* he sends his two sons to Troy to tend the Achaean army. Then his reputation grew and his legend began to take shape: he was the son of Coronis, a Thessalian princess, and Apollo, but his mother had to marry while she was carrying him in her womb and so Artemis, sister of Apollo, fired a deadly arrow at her; Apollo managed to snatch the child from the young woman's bosom. Asclepius was then entrusted to the care of Chiron, the wisest of the Centaurs, who was also the teacher of Achilles and Jason. In his cave on Mount Pelion, Chiron taught him his secrets of healing; Asclepius made such rapid progress in the art of medicine that he was able to

restore the dead to life. Zeus, disturbed by his power, put an end to his exploits by striking him with a thunderbolt. Asclepius was thus not a god, since he was mortal; but he was more than a hero, because even when dead he could still cure. For the purposes of the sanctuary it was decided that Coronis,

while travelling with her father, had been seduced by Apollo at Epidaurus and that the child had been born and passed his early years here, nurtured by a goat and guarded by a dog. From the sixth century BC until the end of the pagan era, the sanctuary enjoyed increasing popularity. If the ruins give little idea of its original aspect, the models in the museum provide an impression of the mass of edifices that covered the valley, dating mostly from the fourth century BC: temples, porticos, propylaea, altars, baths, a palaestra, dormitories, a gymnasium, library, prytaneum (public hall) and stadium. For the Greeks the small area occupied by the sanctuary was a combination of Lourdes and Vichy, and on its great days it was filled with the bustling activity of a vast religious fair. Stelae and *ex-voto* offerings record astounding miracles: a blind man who recovered his sight, a dumb man who was enabled to speak but whom the god then deprived of speech because he had not made an adequate offering, a woman who had been pregnant for five years and finally experienced the joys of childbirth. All this skulduggery on the part of the priests

might seem grotesque, but is not credulity still being exploited today on a similar scale?

The pilgrims approached the sanctuary full of fervour, purifying their bodies and souls before making their sacrifice to the god. Theirs was a spiritual adventure in which hope, faith and the search for purity intermingled. They slept in a dormitory where, during their sleep, they were cured after a dream in which they saw Asclepius come to them, touch them, treat the diseased parts of their bodies or indicate the remedy they should use on awakening. This therapy of the imagination soon developed into more positive methods of treatment. Baths and hydrotherapy establishments were built, and Epidaurus became a watering-place and health resort where people could receive the attention of enlightened physicians whose cures proved as effective as the miracles of Asclepius, if not more so. Indeed, Epidaurus played its part in the history of medicine. Towards the middle of the fifth century BC, like Cos and Pergamum, the 'branches' of this sacred resort, Epidaurus was dominated by the spirit of scientific observation and

generous humanism expressed by Hippocrates in his oath:
'Whatever house I enter, I shall go there for the well-being
of the sick, refraining from all injustice and deliberate mis-
demeanour, especially from the seduction of women and
boys, whether slave or free.'

From the point of view of architecture and decoration,
Epidaurus is interesting in two respects. First of all, it poses
the problem of the *tholos*, the marble rotunda of which a few
traces have survived and which is believed to have been
built towards the middle of the fourth century BC by Polycletus the Younger. This temple possessed two circular
colonnades, the outer colonnade comprising twenty-six
Doric columns, the inner fourteen Corinthian columns; but
its most original feature was its partitioning of six concentric walls, the three nearest the centre forming a spiral
labyrinth. Since the purpose of this edifice is not known,
archaeologists have had to use their imaginations. Some
have seen it as the place where the sacred serpents were
kept, others as an Archaic sanctuary of sacrifice; a recent
theory suggests that the building was designed in imitation
of a mole-hill and that the name Asclepius derives from the
Greek word for mole (*skalops*), an animal which, like all
others living underground, was associated with the forces of
the underworld; the temple would thus represent a zoo-
morphic tradition of earlier date than the cult of the healer-
god.

At Epidaurus one can now see only the foundations of the
Temple of Asclepius, also dating from the middle of the
fourth century BC, but the National Museum in Athens
contains the most precious fragments of its sculptured decoration. The Amazons and Nereides, their sensual, quivering
forms emphasized by the wind flattening their tunics
against their bodies, are believed to be the work of
Timotheus; whatever their origin, they herald a new style
of realism in Greek sculpture.

The greatest miracle of Epidaurus is its theatre, one of
the most powerful and moving expressions in stone of man's
ability to create beauty, and equalled only by our finest
cathedrals. Built in the fourth century by Polycletus the
Younger, it seems to be coiled into the hillside like an
enormous fossil. Fifty-five rows of seats separated in two
concentric zones by a promenade, and divided into equal
sections by fourteen aisles, form an abstract design whose
tautly balanced lines create an overwhelming effect of perfection. In the centre of the orchestra a stone marks the site
of the altar of Dionysus round which the chorus sang and
danced to the sounds of the flute. It is sometimes forgotten
that an ancient comedy or a tragedy was for a long time an
entertainment rather similar to an opera. The actors,
whose increasingly important role finally led to the disappearance of the chorus in the Hellenistic period, performed on a stage built against the *proskenion*, a portico between the columns of which the scenery was changed.

The theatre at Epidaurus, like all the great architecture
of the world, pyramids, temples or cathedrals, is an expression of subtle mathematical relations that make it not only
a work of beauty but also a demonstration of human knowledge. Plato, like Leonardo da Vinci, thought that beauty
and knowledge were identical values. J Bousquet has
identified certain elements of this mathematical design:
thus, the number of tiers is 55, of which 34 are below the
diazoma or circular promenade, and 21 above it. Calcul-
ating the ratios 55/34 (1:617) and 34/21 (1:619), one
realizes that the smaller of these numbers is to the greater
what the greater is to their sum; in other words, the number
55 is divided into its extreme and mean ratio. It will also be
observed that these two ratios enclose the 'divine proportion' or 'golden mean': 1:618.

The theatre of Epidaurus is the most beautiful and best-
preserved of all Greek theatres; in its nakedness it offers
something better than a dramatic entertainment – a sublime moment, face to face with the mysterious marriage of
man and the world.

On a stormy day, under a black sky streaked with lightning, **Mycenae** is a fantastic sight; one expects to see, rising above the sombre ruins, the giant silhouette of Cronos devouring his children with haggard eyes and bloody mouth, the subject of one of Goya's most terrifying nightmares. Even under the brilliant light of summer, a first view of these Cyclopean walls and of the rocky spur which they enclose conjures up a history of anguish and tragedy. After the sublime beauty of the theatre at Epidaurus, Mycenae provides a startling contrast, a testimony to the savagery and violence of primitive times. The Atridae certainly chose the right setting for their deeds. The legend is that Mycenae was founded by Perseus before it fell into their power. Pelops, who has already been mentioned in connection with Olympia, had three sons; the two elder sons, Atreus and Thyestes, banished for having killed their younger brother, took refuge at Mycenae, whose king appointed Atreus as his successor. A deadly hatred now separated the two brothers. Atreus murdered the three sons of Thyestes and, having their bodies cut into pieces, served them to his brother at a banquet. The story went on as it had begun. Their descendant Agamemnon, one of the heroes of the *Iliad,* and his dreadful family were to become one of the most popular of Greek myths, thanks to the genius of Homer. The main episodes of his legend are well known: the sacrifice of his daughter Iphigenia; the adultery of Clytemnestra, his wife, with his cousin Aegisthus while, as King of Kings, he was commanding the Greek army at the gates of Troy; his murder by the two lovers on the evening of his return; the revenge of Orestes and Elektra who killed their mother, Clytemnestra; and the pursuit of Orestes by the Erinyes, the divinities of vengeance, until the pardon was finally obtained by the eloquence of Apollo. This theme was to inspire the three great tragedians, Aeschylus, Sophocles and Euripedes. Aeschylus, in particular, endowed it with a sombre magnificence; the *Oresteia,* performed in 458 BC, was probably his last work and is the only Greek trilogy to have survived intact. The Greek audiences attended performances of all three plays in the same day, with one or two comedies as well. In the *Agamemnon,* the first play of the trilogy, Cassandra, daughter of Priam and the prisoner of the King of Kings, cries out in terror as soon as she arrives at Mycenae, for her gift of prophecy has warned her of the crime that is about to be committed:

CASSANDRA
Apollo, into what fearful house have you led me?
CHORUS
Into the palace of Atreus, as if you did not know . . .
CASSANDRA
Nay, rather a house cursed by the gods, a house that is the accomplice of endless crimes, of crimes which have shed the blood of brothers . . . There are severed heads and limbs, a human slaughter-house

streaming with blood . . .

CHORUS

The stranger, it seems, has the nose of a dog, for she scents blood.

CASSANDRA

I see children weeping under the knife blade and then served as food to their father. But, ye gods, what is now being planned? What terrible suffering is to appear again in this palace? . . . A cruel, intolerable murder which calls for vengeance; but help is far away . . . O horror!

These Mycenaean myths were not the spontaneous invention of the poetic imagination of Homer; the Trojan War certainly took place. Towards the end of the last century a German, Heinrich Schliemann, a scholar, visionary and man of action who, having made his fortune by the age of thirty, devoted the rest of his life to archaeological studies in Greece, was to reveal to the world the Mycenaean or 'Achaean' civilization (it was

Homer who gave the Greeks the name 'Achaean'). The excavations undertaken by Schliemann at Troy (1870), Mycenae (1874) and Tiryns (1884) unearthed the strongholds in which this warrior people lived and the tombs in which it buried its kings and princes. 'Mycenae rich in gold', as Homer called it, delivered up its treasures, a vast quantity of weapons, earthenware and jewellery of stunning workmanship.

Like the medieval *chansons de geste*, the *Iliad*, which must have assumed its written form in the ninth century BC, was a poetic transposition of events that had taken place several centuries earlier. The fall of Troy probably occurred about 1180 BC. Homer was not indulging in fantasy, but investing tradition with the splendour of his genius. If no other work of literature – except for the Scriptures – has ever played as important a role in the moral and spiritual formation of a people as the *Iliad* and the *Odyssey*, this is because the Greeks found in this sublime poetry the history of their ancestors and the expression of the most fundamental values of their race: as Nietzsche observed, Ulysses is the archetype of the Greek man. Seven cities claimed to have been the poet's birthplace. (Fate has decreed that the lives of the two greatest poetic geniuses in the history of humanity, Homer and Shakespeare, should remain shrouded in mystery.) It has been suggested that the *Iliad* and the *Odyssey* were not written by the same author, or that they were a spontaneous creation of the popular genius – but it is the philologists who argue about such things. Even in ancient times the unit and cohesion of these two epics were emphasized by Aristotle. In certain sublime passages – the meeting of Ulysses and Nausicaa, to mention the most

famous – the layman can detect, beneath the colourful simplicity of the images, an acute sensibility and a mocking irony which are the very personality of the poet.

The bands of Achaean warriors must have begun their incursion into Greece by the year 2000 BC; an Indo-European people from the Balkans, they were gradually to take possession of the entire peninsula and establish themselves in force in the Peloponnesus. They also settled in Crete, where the fall and destruction of Knossos (Cnossus) around 1400 BC seem to have

been their doing. The Achaeans were the first Greek invaders of Hellas, fierce and barbarous warriors of the long-headed type who acquired more gentle and refined habits through contact with the Cretan civilization. It is thus known that by the fifteenth century BC, both in Crete and at Mycenae, Greek was already being spoken, though obviously a very primitive Greek; in 1953 two English scholars, M Ventris and J Chadwick, succeeded in deciphering the Achaeans' system of writing, known as 'Linear B' and derived from the Cretan 'Linear A'. This

system was a syllabary of about ninety signs, ill-adapted to the phonetics of Greek and clearly invented for a language of a different structure, probably Cretan, which still remains a mystery. From the tablets found at Pylos and Knossos, and which consist of inventories, it is known that the Achaean nobles had their accounts kept by scribes and supervised the activities of their workmen; a well-developed social structure thus existed by this time. The life of these feudal lords, however, was primarily wild and warlike: their chief occupations were forays against neighbouring towns, expeditions to more distant parts, raids for women and cattle, and hunting lions and wild bulls. More adventurous than the Cretans, they conquered Rhodes and Cyprus, established a footing on the coast of Asia at Miletus and Colophon, traded with Syria and Egypt, and made contacts with the Hittite kings of Anatolia. The Achaean technique of bronze-working appears to have penetrated as far as Sicily and Italy.

At this same period a syncretic tendency was evident which proved decisive for the religious future of Greece: the predominance of female idols and the absence of temples seem to indicate that the religion of Mycenae differed little from that of Crete. On the other hand – the tablets confirm Homer on this point – the Achaeans superimposed on the ancient 'chthonian' or underworld cults a succession of 'heavenly' divinities (*Ouraniones*) who, by the power of their personalities, were soon to supplant the original deities. The most important names of the Olympian pantheon, such as Zeus, Hera, Dionysus and Demeter, have been deciphered from the tablets.

Although the funeral rites of Patroclus and Hector, as described by Homer, have numerous features in common with the rites suggested by archaeological study, there is a fundamental difference: in the *Iliad* the bodies are cremated, whereas the Mycenaean kings, queens and their children were buried in tombs. The bones found in the tombs were covered with gold and with those wonderful masks which some experts regard as the first manifestation of an original Indo-European plastic art. As Pierre Demargne has suggested, this discrepancy can probably be explained by the fact that the Homeric poems, written three hundred years after the great Mycenaean age (thirteenth and twelfth centuries BC), 'reflect a change of ritual due to the influence of Asia Minor and, in particular, to the practice of the Hittite kings'.

At Mycenae and at Tiryns, artistic expression and decorative technique were copied entirely from Cretan art. The subjects of the mural frescoes (dolphins and octopuses) are identical but often more rigid in their lines. Similarly, incised weapons, earthenware and gold jewellery betray the elegance and delicacy of Minoan art. In pottery, also inspired by the delicious naturalism of Crete, one discerns at the same time a fondness for abstraction characteristic of the Indo-Europeans and which seems to foreshadow the Geometric period of Greek art, though the latter did not appear until several centuries later.

In architecture, however, the Achaeans asserted their personality with powerful effect. The enclosure-walls and casemates of Cyclopean masonry, and the doorways framed by colossal blocks of stone, present a military architecture of a size and strength alien to the Cretan palaces. In enlarging their dwellings, the Achaean kings had preserved the traditional design (the double-sloped roof was a survival from the rainy countries from which they had originated). The royal *megaron* comprised a courtyard, an entrance vestibule and a main hall with its central hearth surrounded by four columns – a palace that seems almost like the living-room of an old farmhouse as Nausicaa says to Ulysses: *Cross the great hall and go straight to my mother; in the glimmer of the fire you will see her sitting at the edge of the hearth, with her back to the pillar, while on his seat, in front of the burning fire, my father, like a god, sips his wine.*

Some archaeologists regard the use of semi-columns as foreshadowing the first Doric columns, and the plan of the *megaron* as the model for that of the later temple. At all events, the architecture of Mycenae was the first original manifestation of Greek art, though one must not forget that the Dorian invasion was to cast centuries of darkness and decadence over this achievement; it was only after passing through a period of archaism, with its return to the most primitive forms, that Greek civilization enjoyed a new awakening.

Though the visitor will inevitably be much impressed by the acropolis, the palace-fortress of Mycenae, with the monumental Lion Gate (fourteenth century BC), the Royal Circle of tombs (seventeenth century BC) excavated by Schliemann, and the cistern which is reached by an underground staircase of a hundred and one steps, the undisputed masterpiece of Mycenae lies a few hundred yards away: the *tholos* (circular chamber) known as the Treasury of Atreus or the Tomb of Agamemnon (fourteenth century BC). An open *dromos* (access passage) thirty-six metres long and six metres wide, bordered by a wall of magnificent dressed stones, leads to a monumental doorway flanked by two semi-columns of stone and covered by an enormous lintel. The great shock comes as you enter the tomb, a beehive of stone which has an elegance of line and a harmony of proportion that are quite breathtaking (13·20 metres high, 14·50 metres diameter). This is the most beautiful architectural monument to have survived from the Mycenaean age (called the Late Helladic period, 1580–1100 BC); its contents are now in Athens.

From Mycenae the view extends to the sea, embracing the plain of Argolis. It was here that Io, the beautiful princess loved by Zeus, was running when the jealous Hera changed her into a heifer, entrusting her to the care of Argus, the guardian with the hundred eyes; Hermes managed to close all his eyelids by playing his flute; then Hera fixed a gad-fly to the wretched Io's side and the fly tormented her so cruelly that she fled across the whole of Greece, finally throwing herself into the strait separating Europe and Asia which thereafter was called the Bosporus (meaning 'the passage of the cow').

Corinth, which you can visit before returning to Athens, was one of the most powerful and prosperous cities of Antiquity. What remains today of its past greatness? The seven Doric columns of the Temple of Apollo, an Archaic sanctuary of the sixth century BC, which have remained upright, in spite of invasions, pillage and earthquakes, amid the poppies and wild flowers; the ruins of the Roman city built by Julius Caesar 200 years after the wholesale plundering of the ancient city by the proconsul Mummius (146 BC); and, most interesting of all, an excellent museum which the lover of antiquities must not fail to visit, for it reveals the splendour and refinement of Corinthian pottery in the seventh and sixth centuries (decorated with animal and plant motifs in an Oriental style, the pottery was exported to all parts of Hellas). The museum also contains interesting objects of the Roman and Byzantine periods.

A crossroads between the mainland and the Peloponnesus, and between the Aegean and Ionian seas, Corinth controlled the main communication routes of Greece. The site was occupied as early as the first millennium BC and by the Archaic period the city was already wealthy. Two families, the Bacchiadae and then the Cypselidae, exercized an enlightened tyranny. In the eighth century BC Corinth founded the colonies of Corcyra (Corfu) and Syracuse. In the seventh century, when its commercial activity reached its zenith, its bronze-ware and, in particular, its pottery were sent to every corner of Greece. The collapse of the ruling tyranny at the beginning of the sixth century brought about its political decline. Although Corinth was to remain the enemy of its triumphant rival, Athens, with which it formed an alliance against Sparta only in 395 BC, its prosperous and cautious merchants tried to avoid involving the city in the conflicts of Greece. It continued to amass riches, which eventually aroused the envy of the Romans and led to its systematic pillage by Mummius, when hundreds of ships left for Rome heavily laden with works of art; it was on this occasion that the proconsul is supposed to have said to one of his soldiers, in all seriousness: 'And if you break one statue, I shall make you produce another.'

It is interesting to note that this city, eager for wealth and comfort, inhabited by shrewd merchants who took every advantage of their privileged situation, but who proved singularly lacking in enterprise from the sixth century onwards, produced not a single great sculptor, poet or philosopher. The Corinthians were the Swiss of the ancient world, though it is to be hoped that our Helvetian friends will not suffer the same fate.

Corinth is dominated by the Acrocorinth, a rock over two thousand feet high which was a strategic point of the first importance in ancient times; powerfully fortified by the Byzantines, it was to be occupied by the usual succession of Franks, Venetians and Turks. On the rock there

once stood a small temple of Astarte, a goddess of Phoenician origin identified with Aphrodite; the temple's annexe, a sacred brothel inhabited by a thousand priestess-courtesans and famous throughout the ancient world, was the origin of the Roman proverb: 'Not everyone can go to Corinth' (*non licet omnibus adire Corinthum*).

Not far away, at Isthmia, are the ruins of the Temple of Poseidon, of a theatre and of a stadium which was the scene of the most famous games in Hellas after those of Olympia. The young hero Bellerophon was supposed to have flown from Isthmia on his winged horse, Pegasus, to kill the Chimaera, a fire-breathing monster comprising the extraordinary mixture of a serpent for a tail, a lion's body and a goat's head.

The Corinth Canal (6,343 metres long, 23 metres wide, 8 metres deep) was constructed between 1882 and 1893 by the French and the Greeks, following the layout of the canal begun by Nero and Vespasian. As early as the seventh century BC, the ancients had laid a paved way (*diolkos*) with two parallel grooves on which waggons could be pushed to carry ships across the Isthmus.

3 Aegina The Meteora Rhodes and Crete

The crossing from Piraeus to the island of Aegina takes little more than an hour. If you go by the boat that serves the islands, you will land in the harbour of the little town of Aegina; but if you take one of the daily tourist boats, you will come into the bay of Haghia Marina (it is worth knowing that *haghios*, m. and *haghia*, f. mean 'holy' or 'saint', for you will come across these words at every street-corner). From Haghia Marina you can go up by mule to the Temple of Aphaea; it is quite a steep climb, but there is a beautiful view from the temple, situated at the top of a pine-covered hill; sometimes, in the distance across the sea, you can see the brilliant white of the Parthenon.

On the sacred terrace, which is raised on a stylobate of three steps, stand twenty powerful Doric columns of local limestone, supporting elements of the architrave. Built immediately after the victory of Salamis (480 BC), in which the Aegina contingent had distinguished itself, the temple was dedicated to an ancient local divinity, Aphaea, whose cult was similar to that of the Cretan Artemis-Dictynna and was also associated with that of Athena after the capture of the island by the Athenians in 455 BC. At the beginning of the nineteenth century some wonderful pieces of marble sculpture were discovered which belonged to the two pediments and represented the battle between the Greeks and the Trojans, in a 'heroic' style reminiscent of the pediments of Olympia; bought by the king of Bavaria, they are now in the Glyptothek (museum of sculpture) in Munich. The temple, its simple beauty enhanced by the surrounding pines and the sea, is the only evidence of the glory in Antiquity of this little idland.

In the Mycenaean period Aegina, which was inhabited in Neolithic times, appears to have been called Oinome, a pretty name which it doubtless owed to its vines (*oine* in Greek). During the Dorian conquest immigrants from Thessaly had settled here. According to legend, the island was named after a princess loved by Zeus who had born him a son, Aeacus, the first king of Aegina; a wise and just man, Aeacus was called after his death to join Minos, king of Crete, and his brother Rhadamanthus as one of the three judges of Hades. The poverty of the island encouraged a spirit of enterprise and adventure in its inhabitants, and by the eighth entury BC Aegina, favoured by its position between the Peloponnesus and Attica, had become a busy port trading with Italy, the Middle East, the Black Sea, and Naucratis in Egypt. In the sixth century BC it freed itself from the tutelage of the king of Argos and entered upon its period of greatest prosperity. At the battle of Salamis its thirty ships were in the forefront of the struggle against the Persian fleet. However, the growth of Athenian naval power in the fifth century made it necessary to remove 'this mote which had been blinding Piraeus', as Pericles called the island, and this was done, though not without some difficulty, in 455 BC. Aegina was forced to demolish its fortifications, surrender its ships and pay tribute.

There are other aspects to the history of Aegina. A few kilometres from the town, on the bare slopes of a hill crowned by the ruins of a feudal castle, lies an abandoned city, Paleochora, the capital of the island from the ninth to the eighteenth centuries. During the Middle Ages the cities of the Aegean moved away from the coast to avoid the raids of the Berbers. In spite of the protection of Venice, which kept its hold on the island until 1718 (longer than in any other part of Greece), Paleochora was sacked and destroyed on several occasions, notably in 1537 by the notorious pirate Barbarossa. A stroll among the ruins of the old houses, the monasteries and the ten churches (some of which still have frescoes) offers a rather melancholy charm. Although the only interesting archaeological features of Aegina are a modest museum, the vestiges of its ancient port and a solitary column of a temple of Aphrodite, the town can still look back proudly to its hour of glory at the time of the insurrection and the War of Independence. You can visit the house of one of its heroes, the brave Captain Kanaris. The island's fleet, like that of Spetsai, played an important part in the struggle against the Turks, though neither could dispute the supremacy of another island, Hydra. Liberated at the outset of the insurrection (1821), the town of Aegina was to receive a great many refugees and witness the birth of the modern Greek state, the National Council and the first government of Capodistria.

The **Meteora** are a strange but magnificent sight; these contorted rocks could almost have emerged from the imaginations of the two great Flemish masters of the surreal and the fantastic, Hieronymus Bosch and Patinir. The word 'meteor', meaning 'between heaven and earth', is well suited to the monasteries perched on these gigantic rocks, which assume the forms of pilasters, menhirs, needles and sugar-loaves. The monasteries were built in the fourteenth century AD at a time when war was raging between the emperor of Byzantium and the king of Serbia, who then lived in the neighbouring city of Trikkala, famous in Antiquity as the place where the finest horses in Thessaly were bred. To preserve their solitude and protect themselves against pillage, the holy men planted themselves on the tops of the rocks. Access to the monasteries was provided by wooden ladders which sometimes reached heights of 130 feet, and which could be folded and drawn up; food and animals were hoisted up in nets by means of winches. Today there are steps leading up to the four monasteries still inhabited by a few Orthodox monks: the Meteoron, Haghios Varlaam, Haghia Trias and Haghios Stephanos; soon even these will be deserted, like the twenty other monasteries which are now almost ruined and where hundreds of monks once lived. By the sixteenth century the communities were being undermined by rivalries and corruption; in the eighteenth and nineteenth centuries they were plundered on several occasions. At the top of the broadest rock you can visit the monastery of the Meteoron, founded in 1356 and which, under the protection of the hermit-king Joasaph, son of the emperor of Serbia, was to become the most prosperous and powerful. Its works of art have been stolen or sold, but the church of the Transfiguration still has some beautiful frescoes. Haghios Stephanos, the best-preserved of the monasteries, offering a marvellous

view on to the Pindus mountains, is today occupied by nuns. Haghios Varlaam also contains some fine frescoes and has wooden galleries; it offers accommodation to tourists who find themselves fascinated by this sublime region and who are not too concerned about comfort. Alas, the sublime is no longer daily bread; before long all these monasteries will be deserted.

The town of **Rhodes** is one enormous castle on the sea. It should be seen first from a boat; bathed in the amber light of the sun, the Frankish walls, the palace of the Grand Masters and the minarets suggest some fabulous vision from an Eastern fairy-tale. Here once stood the famous Colossus of Rhodes, the hero and symbol of the city, between whose legs the triremes sailed; this statue of the sun-god, Helios, had a short life: erected in 280 BC, it was destroyed by an earthquake fifty years later. More than a hundred feet high and numbered among the Seven Wonders of the Ancient World, it was not the only one of its kind, for there were a hundred such statues of the solar deity on the island; but these colossi of marble covered with bronze, hardly less

mysterious than the monoliths on Easter Island, have all vanished – the Mediterranean is not a 'pacific' sea.

As one enters the old town, one is immediately transplanted into the Middle Ages; if the eye is not too easily distracted, it will forget the long legs of the young Nordic women and instead will imagine these narrow streets full of knights in armour. This is a truly magnificent ensemble of medieval military architecture: eight huge towers, six giant gateways, four kilometres of fortified walls which, from the fourteenth to the sixteenth centuries, gradually grew stouter until they had reached sixteen metres in thickness; the Hospital of the Knights, now a museum (some exquisite Hellenistic statues of Venus produce a delightful effect in this austere setting); the palace of the Grand Masters and the celebrated Street of the Knights, dotted with the inns occupied by the various communities or *langues*: France, Italy, Provence, Aragon, Castile, England. This ensemble was the work of the Knights of St John, though it was largely restored by Mussolini's architects.

The Knights of St John were, with the Templars and the

Teutonic Knights, one of the three orders established to protect the Holy Places. Founded in Jerusalem in the eleventh century by some merchants of Amalfi, the order soon forgot its bourgeois origins and became a 'club' reserved for the upper nobility. The knights were descended from the greatest families of Europe; titles of nobility had to be proved for four generations, on both the father's and the mother's side, and for eight generations in the case of the German nobility, doubtless considered less reliable. Within its close-knit ranks the order had achieved a united Europe; it was predominantly French and its Grand Masters bore names such as Foulques de Villaret, Pierre d'Aubusson and Villiers de L'Isle-Adam. Compelled to leave the Holy Land in 1291, after their valiant defence of St Jean d'Acre, the Knights of St John were summoned to Rhodes by the Genoese in 1306, at the request of the Pope. They tried to persuade the emperor of Byzantium to give them the island in fief and, when he refused, seized possession of it (1309). For the next two hundred years they were to make life difficult for the Infidels. As the great historian Gibbon observes, with typically Anglo-Saxon irony: 'The Knights neglected to live, but were prepared to die, in the service of Christ.' Quickly converted to the life of the sea, they became redoubtable pirates, plundering and sinking Berber ships and, after the fall of Byzantium (1453), making rapid and fruitful incursions on the coasts of Asia Minor. One of their ships, the 'great carack', was famous: comprising eight decks built one above the other, armed with a hundred cannons, and its hull protected by six thicknesses of metal sheeting, this was a battleship ahead of its time; it could carry 600 sailors and soldiers and food supplies for several months.

The Turks had made several unsuccessful attempts to capture Rhodes. Then Suleiman the Magnificent, declaring that he who had sown the wind would reap the whirlwind, decided to resort to extreme measures, raising an army estimated at 100,000 men (a figure probably exaggerated by Christian hostorians). The 650 knights of the order of St John, assisted by a few sailors and by the inhabitants of the island, sustained a heroic resistance which Paul Morand evokes in his sparkling prose: 'The German artillery roared in defence of the English redoubt, which was being attacked by the Janissaries; in a word, a wonderful Christian harmony in which nations [langues] merged and peoples united under the banner of the West.' After a siege of six months the town surrendered and on 1 January 1523, having been granted the honours of war by Suleiman, the Grand Master Villiers de L'Isle-Adam and the 180 surviving knights boarded ship and left the island. Except for the forcible enlistment of a number of sturdy young Christians in the corps of Janissaries, the Turkish occupation showed clemency and involved no religious persecution; at this same period, both in Spain and in the Netherlands, the Inquisition was torturing and burning in the name of faith. After a short stay in Sicily, the Knights of St John received from Charles V the island of Malta, where they established themselves in 1530. Since the too-powerful Templars had disappeared at the beginning of the fourteenth century, at the instigation of Philip the Fair, king of France, and the Teutonic Knights had never recovered from the defeat inflicted on them at Tannenberg in 1410, only the Knights of St John remained; after suffering various ups and downs, they still exist to this day, though in many cases the old quarterings of nobility have been replaced by million-dollar fortunes.

The fortifications of Rhodes also witnessed the expulsion of the Ottomans in a surprise attack by the Italians in 1912. The *Chora* occupies the eastern part of the fortified town; a few mosques, the busy little lanes, the stalls of the craftsmen and an aroma of leather and spices give this Turkish quarter its distinctive character; you should come here in the evening and visit an open-air tavern, where you can eat broiled lamb flavoured with marjoram or *doner khebab*, while a man sings an old melody to the accompaniment of a violin and a *bouzaki*. The main street running through the old town is now full of luxury shops where jewellery and furs show that Rhodes has been promoted to the rank of a great tourist centre. Yet the town has a pervasive charm, with its tall plane-trees often tossed about by the wind; the broad moat surrounding the walls contains a herd of deer, which seem almost to be challenging the ghosts of the archers who guarded these battlements centuries ago.

Pindar sang of the birth of Rhodes: born of the loves of Helios, the sun-god, and the nymph Rhodea; the island was the child of the East. It was populated by Cretans in the Minoan age and by Achaeans in the Mycenaean period. The Dorians, who settled there about 1100 BC, founded the three cities of Ialysos, Camiros and Lindos, governed by tyrants and associated with Cos and also with two cities of Asia Minor, Halicarnassus and Cnidus, in the confederacy known as the Dorian Hexapolis. Subjugated for a time to the Persians, the Rhodians joined the first Athenian confederacy in 477 BC. In 408 the three cities decided to build a common capital and the celebrated architect Hippodamus of Miletus drew up the geometrical plan of the city of Rhodes. Allied in turn with Sparta, Athens, the Persians, the Ptolemies of Egypt and then the Romans, Rhodes was to enjoy its greatest commercial and artistic success in the Hellenistic period, from the end of the fourth to the middle of the second centuries BC. Its ideal position made it at this time the principal place of call between the ports of Egypt, Phoenicia and Italy and the cities of Greece and Asia Minor. Its commercial and maritime law was so exemplary that, 300 years later, Augustus adopted it throughout the Roman Empire. Its school of sculpture was renowned and worked as successfully in gigantic bronze figures (the famous

Colossus of Rhodes, attributed to Chares, and the Chariot of the Sun by Lysippus, with the statue of Alexander the Great) as in the more delicate statuary represented by the sensuous little marble figures exhibited in the museum. In Roman times it boasted a famous school of rhetoric where Cato, Caesar and Lucretius came to study. It should also be remembered that the greater part of the celebrated library of Alexandria, to which we owe most of our literary knowledge of Greece, came from Rhodes. After siding with Mark Anthony – the choice of alliances in these troubled times was a perpetual gamble for the small Greek cities – Rhodes was sacked by Cassius. Augustus awarded it the title of 'allied city', and Vespasian incorporated it in the Empire. St Paul visited the city, which became the seat of an important archbishopric. On the division of the Roman Empire, the island was naturally attached to the Empire of the East, and it was to remain under Byzantine domination until 1204, when the Fourth Crusade seized Byzantium and proceeded to found the Latin Empire. Soon afterwards Rhodes came under the tutelage of Genoa which, as has been mentioned previously, appealed for help to the Knights of St John.

Apart from its Hellenistic statuary, often rather academic in form (the enormous, richly decorated altar at Pergamum is supposed to have been largely the work of its artists), Rhodes created a pottery of supreme freshness and grace. As early as the eighth and seventh centuries BC it had distinguished itself with some beautiful vases in an Oriental style whose animal and floral motifs were to influence Corinth. In the sixteenth and seventeenth centuries the craftsmen of Rhodes were making blue and green faience of a brilliance and delicacy equalled only by the Abbasid and Seljukid art of Asia.

Rhodes is a green and fertile island dotted with little white villages, and anyone who lingers there will find it deeply appealing. The emperor Tiberius, who was not a particularly sensitive soul, spent several months' holiday in Rhodes and during this time discovered a tranquillity and happiness that surprised the historian Suetonius. Tourists are usually taken to the valley of Petaloudes, at the bottom of which a torrent tumbles and where, from June to September, millions of brown, yellow and red butterflies flutter amid the scent of thyme and myrtle.

Lindos has an appeal of a different kind. The acropolis, near which lie the remains of a castle of the Knights of St John, overhangs a small harbour whose past importance is evident in the presence of numerous Gothic houses. The propylaea and a wide stairway lined with Doric columns lead to the sanctuary of Athena Lindia (fourth century BC), perched on the rock high above the sea; although these are only ruins, the blend of the white and blue of stone, sky and sea gives one a strange feeling of being in a place unique in the world. The nobility of the scene conjures up an image

of man alone again, facing the universe – amid the perfect silence one almost hears the echo of the beautiful cry of Alcestis: *Ah, may you taste the joy of the light!*

Crete lies in the middle of the arc of islands that link Greece with Asia and separate the Aegean and Mediterranean seas. Its mountainous formation leaves little room for the plains, situated mainly towards the north coast. This large island of wild landscapes was the cradle of one of the most brilliant civilizations of the Bronze Age, a civilization that made a major contribution to the awakening of the Greek world.

It may be worth recalling the customary archaeological chronology of Cretan civilization: Early Minoan, 2700–2000; Middle Minoan, 2000–1580; Late Minoan, 1580–1200 – 'Minoan' being the usual name given to the Bronze Age in Crete. Corresponding to these three Minoan cycles are the terms that serve to classify the three phases of the primitive history of Greece: Early, Middle and Late Helladic.

It is thought that Indo-European invaders from Anatolia landed in Crete at the beginning of the Early Minoan period and merged with the Neolithic populations. By the year 2000 BC Crete appears to have entered upon a phase of rapid development in which its contacts with the Babylonian and Egyptian civilizations played an important part; at a time when continental Europe was still in a state of savagery, it was building cities and boats. The island was divided into a large number of kingdoms whose sovereigns lived in palaces. Towards the middle of the eighteenth century BC, as the result either of an invasion or, more probably, of an earthquake, the palaces were destroyed. Then began what is known as the age of the 'second palaces' (1700–1400 BC), during which the Cretan civilization reached its apogee and displayed an astounding originality. The political unity of the island was achieved during the reign of a priest-king, Minos, whose court occupied the vast palace of Knossos. The Greeks were to transform Minos into a legendary figure, a wise and powerful king who, on his death, became one of the three judges of Hades. In fact, *minos* was probably, like *pharaoh* in Egypt, the hereditary title of the Cretan sovereigns. Certain rooms of the palace were reserved for the cult of the mother-goddess of fertility and fecundity, whose sacred animal attributes were the serpent and the bull. Beautiful statuettes of goddesses and worshippers suggest that this was a gentle and benevolent religion. Towards 1400 BC this dazzling civilization was brutally destroyed by the invasion of the Achaeans who, having settled in Greece at the beginning of the second millennium, were no doubt weary of Cretan supremacy and jealous of its art and its refinement. Later, the Athenians were to give this barbarous incursion a more poetic colouring: their hero, Theseus, son of King Aegeus, slayed the Minotaur – a monster to which, every nine years, as a

THE THRONE-ROOM

tribute, seven youths and seven maidens were sent to be devoured alive – and managed to find his way out of the Labyrinth at Knossos by following the thread left by the king's daughter, Ariadne, whom he had seduced. This legend confirms the sensuality and sexual freedom of the Cretan women of this period, characteristics which are discernible in the statuettes of goddesses with heavy, provocative breasts and in the famous portrait of the *Parisienne*, so named no doubt because of her mischievous, inviting expression. The Minotaur was the son of the queen, Pasiphaē, who had fallen wildly in love with a bull to which she had offered herself by hiding in a wooden cow. Her daughter Ariadne fell into the arms of Theseus as soon as she set eyes on him; and Ariadne's younger sister, Phaedra, succeeded in spite of her tender age in kindling the desire of the Athenian hero, who was to return several years later to take her as his wife. All these women clearly possessed a fiery temperament and were consumed with tempestuous passions which Racine was to express in sublime and chaste verse. It also seems that Theseus was a rather unpleasant character. After being received like a prince by Minos, he abducted his daughter, to whom he owed his life, and then abandoned her at Naxos, his first port of call. The author shares the opinion of Michel Déon, who recounts this legend in his own distinctive fashion, with great verve and poetic insight, in *Le Rendezvous de Patmos,* suggesting that on his return to Athens Theseus deliberately hoisted the black sail, the signal of his death, instead of the white sail, the signal of victory, because he was convinced that his father would commit suicide in his grief; Aegeus did precisely this, throwing himself from the Acropolis, and so Theseus became king of Athens.

But here we must leave the poetic ramifications of legend and return to our fragmentary knowledge of the history of civilizations. Crete, after passing on a part of its cultural heritage to the Achaean conquerors, was invaded once more by the Dorians, who landed around the twelfth century BC. During the early Archaic period (eleventh to eighth centuries BC) the island remained an important economic and artistic centre. Its sculptors created what is known as the 'Daedalic' style, producing bronzes full of energy and life, with faceted surfaces, that paved the way for the great statuary of the Peloponnesus. Daedalus, whose name has been borrowed by archaeologists, was a mythical personage of manifold gifts: the architect of King Minos, he built the Labyrinth at Knossos; an aeronautical engineer, he made some wings so that he could fly away with his son Icarus, who plunged to his death in the waters of the Aegean; also a creative artist, he breathed life and movement into his sculpture.

By the beginning of the sixth century BC Crete had become isolated, withdrawing into itself and ceasing to participate in the Greek adventure. Yet the island was still prosperous and renowned for the courage of its inhabitants, who were to be much sought after as mercenaries in the Hellenistic period. The decline of a civilization, like its birth, is a mysterious thing; it seems that, regardless of their power and wealth, people are also dependent on a soul, which manifests itself only at certain special moments.

Crete was occupied by Caecilius Metellus in the first century BC and united with Cyrenaica; it became a Roman province. Then the island belonged to the Byzantine Empire, until 823 when the Saracens seized it. During this first Muslim occupation, which lasted for more than a century, the city of Khandax was founded, later to become Candia, a name subsequently applied to the whole island. In 961 Crete was again occupied by the Byzantines, who evacuated it in 1204 after the capture of Constantinople by the Fourth Crusade; the Marquis of Montferrat, to whom the island was assigned, sold it to the Venetians who were to rule it for more than four hundred years (1216–1669). At first Venice encountered fierce opposition from the Cretans

and had to suppress several uprisings, but in the sixteenth and seventeenth centuries the island, by this time pacified, enjoyed a great renascence. One of its sons, imbued with the fervour of the Byzantine icon-painters, was to leave for Spain and become an artist of universal renown: Domenikos Theotokopoulos, known as El Greco.

The Turks made themselves masters of the island in spite of the heroic resistance of the capital, Candia, which remained under siege for twenty-three years. For more than two hundred years (1669–1898) the island bore the burden of an Ottoman administration that was often indolent and sometimes cruel. During the nineteenth century four uprisings provoked bloody reprisals. The revolt of 1897 finally brought autonomy to Crete, which was definitively united with Greece in 1913. An exchange of population after the war of 1922 replaced the Turkish Muslim minority with Greek refugees from Asia Minor.

The capital changed its Venetian name of Candia for the less graceful but more heroic name of Heraklion or Iraklion, which means 'the place of Hercules'. It is not a particularly attractive town, but has the advantage of being able to offer comfortable hotels. Little remains of its ten centuries of turbulent history, though it has a fine Venetian fountain named after one of the greatest captains of the city of the doges, Francesco Morosini, who in the seventeenth century vigorously defended the Greek cities subject to the Venetian Republic, such as Corinth, Nauplia and Aegina, when they were attacked by the Turks. At Candia, however, he had little success; arriving in 1667, he was forced to withdraw on 5 September 1669, after his troops had suffered terrible losses. The 6,000 French soldiers sent by Louis XIV in 1668 stayed only a few months in the besieged town; they reembarked after making a sortie that proved disastrous and cost them the life of their leader, the Duc de Beaufort, the natural grandson of Henry IV of France and who earned the title *Roi des Halles* ('King of the Markets') during the Fronde rebellion.

If Heraklion is a town of no great charm, it is nevertheless the key that opens the door to the fascinating discovery of the Cretan civilization. Five kilometres from the town lies the palace of **Knossos.** In Heraklion itself, near one of the walls of the Venetian fortifications, there is a museum which contains some wonderful exhibits – fragments of frescoes, vases, jewels and sculptures. At first the eye is dazzled by the sheer invention and sensitivity of this Minoan art, then one is filled with an overwhelming awareness of its profound beauty. The excavation of Knossos (Latin spelling Cnossus) was begun in 1900 by Sir Arthur Evans. Schliemann would certainly have forestalled Evans if he had not been refused permission by the Turkish authorities. The restoration work of the British archaeologist has often been criticized. Concrete was then a new material and was often misued. The exterior paintings and the copies of the frescoes sometimes

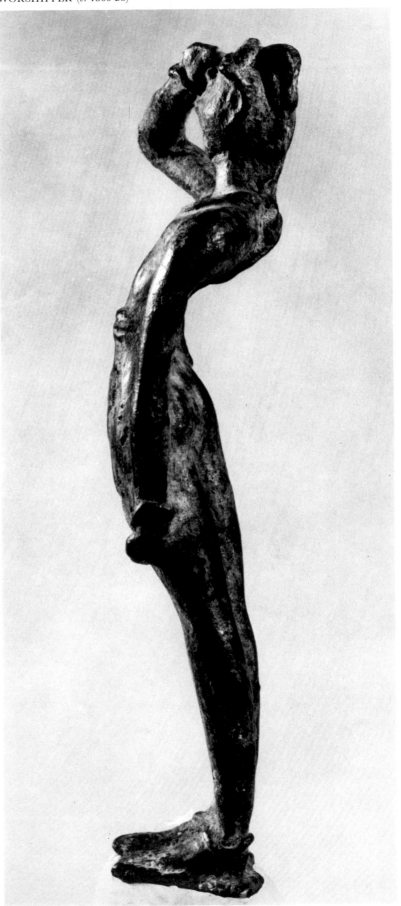

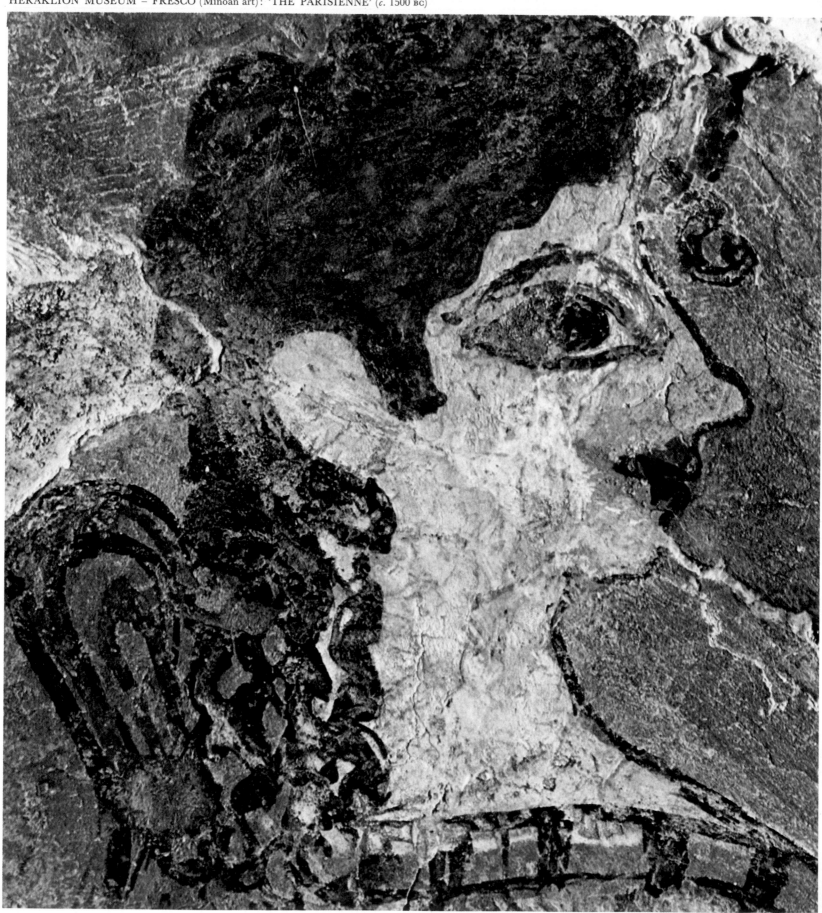

FRESCOE: BULL AND ACROBAT (*c.* 1500 BC)

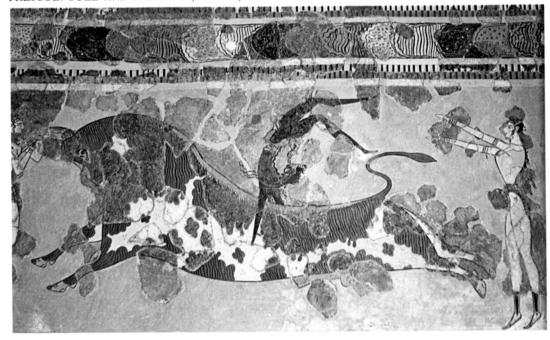

suggest artifice – but how could this have been otherwise? The work was certainly carried out with great care and respect; a partial restoration, even if it does not satisfy everyone, is a very useful aid to the imagination.

Knossos, situated a few kilometres from the sea in an undulating and fertile region, must have numbered 80,000 inhabitants at the height of the Minoan monarchy. The palace is built around a large central courtyard; it was enlarged on numerous occasions and, before its destruction, comprised nearly 1,800 rooms. Seen from an aeroplane, its structure resembles the cells of a beehive, a feature which it shared with the Neolithic cities of Anatolia and Mesopotamia. At the various stages of its construction the palace consisted of two, three or four storeys, sometimes with underground crypts. The Athenian legend of the Labyrinth built by Daedalus is easy to understand, for even in its ruined state the palace is a complicated structure where the visitor can soon get lost. On the west side of the rectangular courtyard were the official rooms: the sanctuary, the votive chamber and the throne-room with its famous alabaster throne and the counsellors' bench; behind this first block of buildings, occupying two or three storeys, were the storerooms. The royal apartments stood along the east side of the court and comprised the king's megaron and the queen's megaron, with a bathroom decorated with a fresco of dolphins; behind the apartments lay the servants' quarters and the workshops of the royal craftsmen (stone-cutters, goldsmiths, etc.). All these disparate elements were assembled like cubes, in no apparent order, linked by corridors, passages and staircases, lit on the outside by windows and on the inside by light-wells. The roofs were flat and the façades had numerous recesses. Painted columns of brick or wood were sometimes placed in the centre of the rooms and also supported verandahs, balconies and galleries built across the

hillside and connecting buildings at different levels. The walls of rather crude stones were covered with stucco and often decorated with frescoes or painted reliefs. There can be no doubt that, both in architecture and in decoration, the Cretans were largely dependent on Egyptian or Mesopotamian techniques. At the time when Hammurabi reigned at Babylon (seventeenth century BC) Knossos had close links with several Syrian cities, such as Mari, Byblos and Ras Shamra

(Ugarit), by which it was undoubtedly influenced.

The palace of Minos is typically Mediterranean. It was built for the pleasure of a monarch who, confident of his power, had no need to surround himself with military fortifications; as far as hygiene and toilet facilities were concerned, its comforts were vastly superior to those of the Versailles of Louis XIV 3,000 years later.

Only a careful study of the **Museum of Heraklion** can enable one to

appreciate the variety, freedom and invention of Cretan art. Of the original frescoes, executed in distemper on damp stucco, there remain only fragments, which were completed by the restorers in a deliberately visible manner. Everywhere the visitor is confronted with marvels: the celebrated acrobat leaping over a bull's horns, scenes of dancing, processions and ritual offerings, figures of monkeys, birds and dolphins, or painted reliefs such as the Prince of the Lilies and the magnificent bull's head; in all these works the perfect observation of nature is combined with a startling freshness and spontaneity. Crete produced no colossal statuary in the manner of Egypt and Mesopotamia; only small figurines twenty to thirty centimetres high have been discovered, goddesses, worshippers and animals fashioned in a variety of noble materials – bronze, ivory, faience, black diorite and stucco – and in which realism is sometimes tinged with sensuality or grotesque humour. The pottery, with its simple decorative themes (flowers, fish, octopuses, birds), varied shapes and beautiful colours (metallic blue, olive green, red-brown),

is probably the domain in which the Minoan artists most vividly expressed their imaginative power and zest for life. The gold jewellery has an astounding elegance and was also inspired by naturalist themes, such as bees or lotus blossom. The excavations at Knossos revealed some masterpieces of gem-engraving – seals of agate, cornelian and onyx, often depicting rustic scenes (a cow suckling its calf, a male and a female goat copulating). The gold-smiths of the Renaissance were to equal this technical perfection, but they could not achieve such natural and poetic effects on tiny surfaces.

At the time of its discovery at the beginning of the twentieth century, Cretan art aroused the interest of painters such as Bonnard and Roussel, sculptors such as Bourdelle, ceramists and glassware artists such as Gallé and Lalique. Its delicate grace and its frescoes with their flat tints of brilliant colours became distinctive features of the decorative style adopted by the Russian Ballet.

By its own radiance and, later, through the conquests of the Achaeans, Minoan art certainly influenced and

enriched the whole of Hellas, but three centuries of darkness appear to have followed the Dorian invasion of the twelfth century BC. When an original art finally emerged once again around the ninth century BC, the brilliant past of Crete had been forgotten and it was only by reverting to the most primitive forms that Greece gradually achieved the mastery of technique that led her to artistic glory.

It must be emphasized, moreover, that Cretan and Greek art reflect two distinct types of mind and sensibility. Greek art is, above all, order and balance the predominance of lines and volumes to express the essential. Minoan art, as can be seen in the palace architecture and its lack of any precise discipline, seems to have adapted itself to a natural development; the paintings and sculptures owe their splendour to an exuberance and a freshness, a relish for nature and a sensuousness, which Greece was never to display, except perhaps in her decline during the Hellenistic period. Worshipping a fertile and pacific mother-goddess similar to the divinity of the Neolithic cities of Asia Minor,

the Cretan civilization was profoundly susceptible to the imagination and to the joy of life, revealing an almost feminine sensitivity. In contrast, the Greek civilization, a product of warrior peoples, the Achaeans and Dorians, and epitomized by the figure of Zeus, the god of the thunderbolt, of vengeance and of courage, found its ideal of beauty in order, dignity and virility.

If you are not pressed for time you should go to **Phaestus**, situated near the south coast of the island about fifty kilometres from Heraklion; the road runs through the hills dominated by Mount Ida, the highest mountain in Crete (2,148 metres). In one of its many caves Zeus was supposed to have been born and then rescued from the voracious appetite of his father, Cronus, by his mother, Rhea, though numerous other mountains claim the same honour. The majestic ruins of Phaestus lie over the plain of Hieropotamus, which runs down to the sea and the gulf of Messara. The remnants of palaces, which have been excavated but not restored, lie scattered over the ground; the blocks and slabs of stone are more massive than at Knossos and not much different from those employed in Greek architecture. A few kilometres away, in an entrancing setting, is the little palace of Haghia Triada. It was amid the awe-inspiring surroundings of Phaestus that Henry Miller experienced his revelation; in *The Colossus of Maroussi* his lyrical prose glorifies this ideal meeting-place of man and the universe. Here, in an intense silence, he felt the heart of the world beating and was filled with an ecstatic happiness. The brilliance and wild mystery of Crete invite such excesses and one can only regret that the great modern novelist Nikos Kazantzakis has not been able to give expression to this extravagance. In spite of their heroic themes, *Christ Recrucified* and *Zorba the Greek* are picaresque novels.

Ideally one should discover Crete with a haversack on one's back at the age of twenty, for this country still offers the traveller a great adventure that requires physical agility and a capacity for enthusiasm. The romantic image of the Cretan – the broad belt with its silver pistols, the black turban, baggy trousers and scarlet leather boots – has not become totally divorced from reality. Crete has remained faithful to its traditions, and if piracy and brigandage have gradually vanished, the heroism of its people, oppressed for centuries, wronged, defeated and yet always rebellious, has not diminished – as the Germans discovered during the last war. The Cretans' sense of honour, what is called on the island *levendia*, can be compared only to the Spanish *pudonor* or the Sicilian *omerta*; but the Cretans do not have the sensitivity of the Spaniards or the suspiciousness of the Sicilians, and their rough bonhomie is expressed well enough in a couplet of one of those *mandinathas* that they are always singing:

> *Courage is man's only true wealth,*
> *To drink, eat and take the best from life.*

4 The Islands

To visit the islands is to discover the true character of Greece – expanses of land and rock saturated with light, enveloped by sky and sea. Unhindered by the detailed historical information necessary when going to the major sites, such as Delphi, Olympia and Mycenae, the traveller can share the simple Greek way of life which, in certain places, has not changed since Antiquity. On these islands ruins are forgotten but the past remains very much alive; here one can still find the spirit of equality, the uncomplicated and peaceful existence, which must have prevailed in the Homeric age thirty-five centuries ago.

Except when visiting the sanctuary of Apollo on Delos, which requires a certain background knowledge, one should not explore the islands with guide-book in hand, but wander at leisure and with an open heart – the only books one needs are a copy of the *Odyssey* and an anthology of Greek poetry.

It is the chance encounter that best reveals the dignity and generosity of these Greek people, who are often reserved but will suddenly open up like a flower. The warmth of the *'yasou!'* exchanged when clinking two glasses of *retsina* is not just a convention but a genuine wish of happiness. These folk have remained open-hearted; the peasant-woman met at the roadside will hold out a fistful of figs or a bunch of grapes, a modest but gracious gift of human friendship, and the old shepherd to whom you offer a cigarette will give you a simple and friendly 'thank you' with his eyes. The world has lost this language, but in Greece it still remains, a survival from a distant age. In Homeric times, it seems, warrior instincts existed side by side with a way of life of astonishing simplicity and nobility: kings were labourers and princesses washerwomen. Is not the achievement of a civilization measured primarily by its success in establishing harmony in human relations?

Today the islands are being subjected to the assault of progress; money, noise, bad taste and self-interest are establishing their tyranny here as in other parts of the world. Amid all this false glitter, how can one hope to resist the temptations of comfort and profit and to safeguard this ancient balance of wisdom and dignity? On the little islands, however, far from the invading hordes, one can still find intact the natural qualities of the heart. According to individual temperament, the visitor will discover here either the vestiges of a paradise that has been irrecoverably lost, or the sign of man's vocation and a reason to hope in his future destiny.

The islands form a bridge between Greece and Asia; it was through them that Eastern influence penetrated to the mainland to provide the catalyst of Greek civilization. The art of the Cyclades and, in particular, the art of Crete possessed a refinement which continental Greece was to take centuries to discover, and which in many respects she was never to equal. The proximity of Asia Minor, Mesopotamia and Egypt proved beneficial to the islands, bringing ethnic intermixtures and commercial exchange, and consequently their populations were for a long time the most enterprising and creative in all Hellas. Seven cities each claimed the honour of being Homer's birthplace – and after reading the *Odyssey*, can one imagine the poet as anything but a child of the islands? In this Ionian archipelago where the human mind proved no less fertile than the soil, many scholars, poets and philosophers were to be born, men such as Thales, Aristarchus, Pythagoras, Protagoras and Hippocrates. In the sixth century BC, under the tyrant Polycrates, the ally of Egypt, Samos became the cultural centre of the Aegean and only Miletus, a city in Asia Minor, could emulate its prosperity and its cultivation of the sciences and the arts.

The map of Greece is a jigsaw puzzle of land and sea; this extremity of Europe breaks up into fragments of various shapes and sizes scattered over the Mediterranean, which is here divided into the Aegean and the Ionian Seas, named in homage to the gods and the heroes. These seas are quite different in character. The Ionian Sea is a continuation of the Adriatic and since ancient times has provided access to southern Italy and Sicily. In winter the sirocco blows, a warm and humid wind from Africa, or the *grēgalē*, a dangerous north wind; in summer the sea is calm and the atmosphere mild. The Ionian islands, Corfu, Zante and Cephalonia, were never occupied by the Turks, but remained subject to Venice until the end of the eighteenth century; they were restored to Greece by Britain in 1862. Although they are closely linked with Homeric legend in the person of Ulysses, supposedly lord of Ithaca, and have always been inhabited by Greeks, the islands are unmistakeably reminiscent of Italy in their green countryside, their soft light and the nonchalant charm of their way of life.

The Aegean Sea, enclosed by the coasts of Greece and Turkey, and bounded to the south by the arc formed by the islands of Kythira (Cythera), Crete, Karpathos and Rhodes, is a vast basin which Berbers, Venetians, Turks and Italians controlled by turns without ever being able to jeopardize its deep-rooted links with Hellas. The miracle of the Aegean is the translucent atmosphere which gives an acute intensity to forms and colours. From May to September the *meltemi* blows from the north, often violently, especially in the middle of the day, and brings fresh breezes to the islands. This wind played an important part in the history of Greek civilization, for it pushed the Greeks towards Crete, Asia and Egypt; in winter the boats were hauled ashore and at the beginning of the following spring returned to the Greek ports before the Etesian winds blew up.

Two main archipelagos occupy the Aegean: the islands of the Dodecanese which, as their name implies, are twelve in number, and the Cyclades, strewn across its centre like a handful of pebbles.

The islands of the Dodecanese border the Turkish coast and some of the larger ones, such as Lesbos, Chios and Samos, are so close to it that they have the same green countryside and red-tiled houses; these islands were not liberated from Turkish occupation until 1912; then the Italians seized Rhodes, which they did not return to Greece until 1948, at the same time as the other islands of the Dodecanese which they had taken during the war of 1912. The populations of the Dodecanese have always been fiercely devoted to the mother country; their revolt at the time of the War of Independence was bloodily suppressed by the Ottomans and the massacre of Chios acquired a gruesome fame. The islands absorbed a large number of Greeks from Asia Minor in the population exchange of 1923, the disastrous sequel to the Greco-Turkish war.

The Cyclades comprise some thirty islands which, as their name indicates, form a circle, the sacred isle of Delos being the historical nucleus of the group and the island of Paros its geographical centre. The Cyclades are mostly bare and rocky; their brilliant white villages of cube-shaped houses stand out against the bright blue sky – at the very heart of Hellas they irradiate light like diamonds and, in the clarity and harmony of their lines, are symbolic of the Greek genius.

Poros, Spetsai and Hydra, near the coast of the Peloponnesus, owe their more active life and more diversified populations to the proximity of Athens. Their pretty harbours are adorned with gaily coloured little houses built in tiers over the hillside, huddling against each other, with the sun shining on their façades of ochre, orange or blue.

The northernmost islands of the Sporades – Skiathos, Skopelos, Thasos, Lemnos and Samothrace – are mountainous and have some fine forests; still relatively undiscovered by tourists, they offer enchanting rocky creeks and vast beaches of sand to those in search of solitude.

Quite independently of their geographical situation, the Greek islands all have their own personalities. There are green islands among the Cyclades – Tinos, Ios, Siphnos – and white and grey islands among the Dodecanese – Patmos, Symi and Kalymnos where the inhabitants fish for sponges. There are wild, mysterious islands such as Kythira, Santorin and Crete, and gay, smiling islands like Skopelos, Corfu and Rhodes. There are even fashionable islands – Mykonos, Paros, Hydra and Spetsai. And then everyone has his own special island: Lawrence Durrell found happiness on Corfu, Michel Déon on Spetsai, Henry Miller on Crete, and many others have discovered their own secret, solitary beach where the vines and olive-trees run down to the sea. In the memory this diversity of scene becomes concentrated to form an ideal, simplified image of the typical Greek island: a dazzling light, the terraces of a hillside rising from the sea to a summit crowned with the ruins of a Frankish castle or of Turkish or Venetian fortifications; on the *kastro* (acropolis), a shimmering church dedicated to St Nicholas, the patron-saint of sailors; not far away, an old mill with motionless sails and a few bits of ancient marble encircled by vines; and on the square, the friendly welcome of a taverna, the hub of the social life of the village.

According to individual temperament, the islands either offer the opportunity of a prolonged stay and the daily contacts which enable one to share their simple and happy way of life; or, in contrast, they invite the visitor to discover their variety and savour their wealth of light, forms and colours. For travelling round the islands the ideal solution is to hire a private yacht, for then one can move about as the fancy takes one, relishing the joys of the unexpected.

A great many tourists visit the islands during the brief calls made by the big cruise ships, which often offer more adventure on board than on land. If you do not care for the

idea of these group excursions and seek a simpler and more authentic atmosphere, you should take one of the steamers that serve the islands regularly, or one of the caiques which transport goods between the islands and which welcome the enterprising traveller.

When setting off from Athens, visitors nearly always forget Euboea, an island over a hundred miles long situated off the east coast of Greece and which seems to belong to the mainland. This is an unfortunate omission, for the island has some marvellous scenery; Chalcis, its attractive capital, was one of the most active Greek cities of Antiquity.

From the harbour of Kini or from that of Volo, or directly from Piraeus, you can easily reach the **Northern Sporades**. Situated a little apart from the rest, Skyros is the main island; its bareness and its white, geometrical houses with their flat roofs are reminiscent of the Cyclades. It was on Skyros that Theseus was supposed to have been treacherously put to death and that Ulysses discovered Achilles, who had been hidden in a woman's clothes by his mother. But the most beautiful of these islands are Skopelos, Alonysos and, in particular, Skiathos, their green and mountainous landscapes resembling Mount Pelion,

which lies opposite (the waterfalls and forests of chestnuts and beeches on Mount Pelion were the home of the unruly Centaurs and of Chiron, the teacher of Asclepius, Jason and Achilles). Skopelos is covered with vines, olives, almond-trees and fruit-trees; its houses have pink and blue walls; the houses of Skiathos are white and roofed with red tiles. The Northern Sporades, unknown to tourists a few years ago, still have some wild and lonely spots; they also possess some wonderful beaches (the beach along the bay of Koukounaries, on the east coast of Skiathos, is considered one of the most beautiful in Greece).

Mount Athos, one of the most fantastic places in Greece, cannot be visited by women or girls; the prohibition also applies to female animals and eunuchs! If, however, you take a boat round the peninsula – thirty miles long and joined to the mainland by a narrow strip about a mile long across which Xerxes cut a canal for his Persian fleet – you will be able to see the majority of its twenty monasteries, set in wild countryside: Simonos Petras, Gregorios, Dionysos and, on the west coast, the Great Lavra, Iviron and Vatopedi. Perched on the cliff-top or over the hillside, the imposing monastery buildings are crowned with red

and gilt domes.

The Great Lavra, founded in the tenth century by Athanasius the Athonian, the friend and counsellor of the emperor Nicephorus Phocas, is the oldest and largest of the monasteries. It possesses a rich treasury comprising a piece of the True Cross, gold and silver objects, and icons which include the famous Panaghia Koukouzelissa (one day, as the monk Koukouzelos was singing in front of the icon, the Virgin handed him a medal; on another occasion, when he sang a wrong note, she gave him the correct pitch). The monastery of Vatopedi, overlooking a beautiful bay, contains the oldest mosaics and icons (eleventh century); according to legend it was built by Arcadius, son of the emperor Theodosius, who as a child, while travelling by boat, was swept overboard by a wave during a storm and was carried by the tide to a raspberry-bush, where the monks found him. The monastery has an enormous library of 8,000 volumes and the richest treasury on Mount Athos, including the jasper cup of Michael Palaeologus and a variety of precious objects donated by John Cantacuzene, tutor of John Palaeologus, who was banished by Palaeologus after usurping the throne of Byzantium and came to end his days in the monastery (fifteenth century). Vatopedi also possesses a miraculous icon, the Panaghia Portaitissa, who enabled the angel Gabriel to walk on the water.

Mount Athos is immersed in legend – it is hardly surprising that the real and the imaginary should have become confused in this mysterious and awe-inspiring place inhabited by hermits who could halt the sun, walk on the waves and tame wild animals with a look. Not so long ago some of these holy men were still spending their lives perched on a column, while others, like St Euthymios, went about on all fours chewing grass. The frontiers of this great

spiritual adventure have diminished, and in the monasteries asceticism has given place to boredom and routine. At one time there were 40,000 monks (*caloyers*) on Mount Athos; today there are barely 2,000. Most of them are cenobites – that is to say, they live in a community and are obliged to fast all the year round and to attend the four daily offices: mass, vespers, compline and the *nykterinos* or night office. But there are also 'idiorrythmic' monasteries where the monks live on their own personal resources without the obligation to fast or attend services. On Mount Athos one finds hermits living in isolated places, and sarabaites, who live in small communities of two, three or four, on the mountainside or by the sea, in solitary dwellings (*kellies*) built against a chapel.

Seventeen of the twenty monasteries on Mount Athos are Greek; the other three, Russian, Serbian and Bulgarian, have their own rites and customs. Each monastery has at its head an *higoumen*. The theocratic republic of Mount Athos, comprising a clearly defined system of hierarchies, comes under Greek sovereignty and is administered from the village of Karyes by the Holy Community, which includes a representative of each monastery. The calendar on Mount Athos is thirteen days behind our Gregorian calendar. The first hour of the day begins at sunrise, except at Vatopedi, which follows European time, and at Iviron, where it begins at sunset. There are no bells on Mount Athos; instead, long pieces of wood are struck with an iron mallet, resounding with grave and powerful tones.

The common idea of Byzantium is a distortion based on the period of its decline and fall, a distortion that stems from an inglorious tradition: on the occasion of the Fourth Crusade (1204) the Franks and the Latins, who had set off to fight the infidel, pillaged the Empire of the East under pretexts that ill concealed their cruelty, am-

bition and greed. It is strange to observe how, psychologically, the break between the Empire of the East and the Empire of the West in the fourth century has lasted to this day. During the twelve centuries of its history Byzantium, which succeeded in keeping the Greek tradition alive, enjoyed times of splendour and glory under the rule of enlightened *basilei*, the all-powerful emperors who controlled both the temporal and the spiritual domains. During this time a burning faith and an intense spirituality pervaded holy places such as Mount Sinai, the valley of Göreme and Mount Athos. Today only the

last-named has survived; even in its decline and despite its blemishes, Mount Athos still bears testimony to the exalted and boundless faith of these inspired men.

In the photographs which he took during a brief stay in Mytilene, the ancient **Lesbos**, Edouard Boubat was able to capture the true atmosphere of the life of the islands. The inhabitants of each of these communities are united by a spirit of solidarity which they owe in part to the poverty and isolation in which they have lived for so long. Their courtesy, dignity and generosity are the heritage of ancient traditions. Their days are occupied with fishing, the cultivation of the vine and of corn, and domestic chores. In the evenings the women sit in front of their houses, chatting with their neighbours; the children play in the lanes or on the quayside; the men sit at café tables, sometimes with only a glass of water in front of them, playing interminable games of dominoes or cards. Teeming with life in the summer months, the villages slumber in boredom and melancholy when winter comes. Only the women pursue their tasks; the houses, carefully whitewashed, are meticulously clean; each

day the children set off for school or church. To break the monotonous rhythm of the seasons there are births, marriages, funerals and the festivals in which everyone takes part. And there is always the unexpected – the return of a son who has been away for several years working on a cargo-boat or a steamer and who has brought back his savings for his sisters' dowries; or the arrival of an 'American', a native of the island who emigrated to the United States to make his fortune and now comes home to end his days in the village of his birth, where he will buy a business or, to parade his wealth, build a frightful 'modern' house. These modest and hard-working people respect money and naïvely regard a fortune as a token of merit. Even among the simplest of the islanders one of the key factors in the choice of a wife is the amount of her dowry.

The traditions of harmony and diversity that for a long time inspired the domestic architecture of the Greek islands have unfortunately vanished (there is a handsome book illustrated by Panos N Djelepy with drawings of these old houses, the style of which

129

varies greatly from one island to another). Intoxicated
with the false glamour of luxury and success, the islanders
are disfiguring their enchanting countryside with hideous
pavilions. In this land where only poverty seems to en-
gender dignity and taste, money is nearly always flaunted
gaudily and offensively.

In recent years tourism has lifted most of the islands out
of the sleepy existence into which they had sunk. In the
nineteenth century, before the powerful shipowners of
Piraeus began to dominate commerce, many of the islands
were engaged in a substantial sea-borne trade of which
almost nothing now remains, except for a few caiques
transporting goods from one island to another. The steadily
increasing waves of summer invaders have resulted in
large-scale tourist development, and the more enterprising
islanders have seized the opportunity to establish various
profitable ventures; houses and land have acquired
exorbitant values – in fact, the whole economy of the
islands benefits in some degree from the feverish activity
of the summer months.

For the time being, however, the majority of the islands
have preserved their ancient character. Among the 'elders'
of the islands – to use Homer's expression, more dignified
than 'old' – one encounters certain faces that seem the
epitome of destiny and fatality, like the masks of ancient
tragedy. Sometimes, groups of women dressed all in black
have an intensity of expression and a strength of features
that remind one of the Erinyes, the deities of vengeance,
who could also, depending on their mood, become the
benevolent Eumenides.

The elderly inhabitants often have a noble and rather
sad gravity which seems to bear testimony to the terrible
ordeals that these islands have suffered: the raids of the
Berbers, the Franks, the Venetians and the Muslims,
centuries of Turkish domination, revolts and bloody
reprisals, not to mention the appalling earthquakes that
destroyed some of the islands; Zante, Cephalonia and

Santorin were ravaged again less than twenty years ago. In 1923, in the exchange of population that followed the disastrous Greco-Turkish war, 1,500,000 Greeks left Asia Minor and settled in large numbers on the islands, especially those of the Dodecanese where many of them lived in misery. The resplendent sun, the deep blue of the sea and the sky, and the dazzling whiteness of the houses seem to radiate a permanent happiness, and one forgets or is unaware that, over the centuries, these islands have experienced anguish, servitude, destitution – all the tribulations of history.

There are two Greek islands that must be visited at all costs, Patmos and Santorin, for they have a splendour and a mystery that distinguish them from all the others. **Patmos**, near Samos, is the most northerly of the Dodecanese group and yet, in its rugged nakedness, the brightness of its light and the whiteness of its cube-shaped houses, it is strongly reminiscent of the Cyclades. You land in the little harbour of Skola, where fragments of ancient columns serve as mooring bollards, and then go up to the delightful village of Chora, the capital, dominated by the white mass of the monastery-fortress of St John

(Haghios Yoannis Theologos), which dates from the fifteenth century but whose origins go back much further, since its construction was one of the conditions on which Alexis Comnenus donated the island to St Christodulus in 1088. From the monastery there is a striking view of the entire island, with the church of Panoya and the houses clustered round it, the deep thrust of the bay of Merika which seems to cut the island in two, and the sea encircling its three volcanic masses. This is a thrilling panorama, wild and yet graceful, a scene of stark simplicity and intense colouring. At first it is difficult to imagine that this island, with its rigorously pure outlines, could have served as the setting for the terrifying visions that the apostle St John transcribed in magnificent images in The Apocalypse, which, with the Book of Ecclesiastes, is the most moving text in the whole of the Old and New Testaments. Arrested at Ephesus and plunged into boiling oil in Rome, Christ's favourite companion is supposed to have ended his days here, in the reign of Domitian, after dictating this book inspired by the Holy Spirit to his pupil Prochorus.

St John was the proudest of all the disciples, but also the most faithful

and generous; his favourite words were 'God is love' and 'Love one another'. The Apocalypse, or Book of Revelation, a work of flames and ashes, is composed of seven visions which, after a succession of dreadful catastrophes and the reign of the Antichrist, predict the final triumph of the Church – the heavens open and the City of God, Jerusalem, descends unpon the earth. The fearsome cataclysms predicted – barbarian invasions, a downpour of rocks, blocks of ice and balls of fire, earthquakes, the explosion of the moon, floods and tidal waves – were probably intended to sow terror and to silence the quarrels and rivalries of the seven churches of Asia: Ephesus, Smyrna, Pergamum, Thyatira, Sardis, Philadelphia and Laodicea.

Half way between Skola and Chora are the chapel of St Anne and the grotto of St John; a young monk will show you the fissure in the rock from which the voice of God issued. The monastery has a more authentic appeal; its situation and its walls protected it from the pirates and the Berbers who, even in the eighteenth century, frequently put into the harbour. The library contains precious Byzantine and Frankish manuscripts,

including fragments of the fifth-century *Codex Porphyrus*, a copy of the Gospel of St Mark on purple parchment illuminated with gold and silver.

Like a rough diamond set in the Aegean Sea, Patmos sparkles with a thousand lights; dominated by the figure of St John, the most tempestuous of the apostles, this island of abstract purity can assume a symbolic value in the eyes of the inspired visitor: 'God is the alpha and the omega, the beginning and the end of all things . . .'

Santorin, the ancient Thera, which owes its modern name to its patroness, St Irene, presents some extraordinary scenes which, in their sheer extravagance, are worthy of the descriptions in The Apocalypse. Towering above the sea, a precipitous cliff 600 feet high, a brutal gash in the earth's crust, reveals the mysteries of geology. Disposed in layers one above the other, and sometimes intermingling in this enormous surface of rock, the schist, scoriae, pumice-stone, black and red cinders, white marble, and lava of green and grey provide a startling spectacle in which the only sign of human life is the white trail of villages perched on the cliff-top. The cliff is the crater-wall of a huge volcano, six miles in diameter, whose centre is now occupied by the anchorage, which is about 1,200 feet deep. The islands of Therasia and Aspronisi are other fragments of the circular wall of this volcano, which appears to have collapsed towards the middle of the second millennium BC, causing a mighty tidal wave that may have been responsible for the destruction of the first Minoan palaces around 1700 BC (Crete is less than sixty nautical miles from Santorin). The volcano remained active beneath the water and over the centuries the islands of Palaia Kaimeni (726), Mikra Kaimeni (1573) and Nea Kaimeni (1711) emerged in the centre of the

bay; the 'Old', 'Little' and 'New' Burnt Islands still emit vapours and smoke; the most recent eruptions occurred in 1925 and 1928, and in 1956 Santorin was ravaged by an earthquake. The capital, Phira, a delightful little white town with pretty lanes, has suffered much; perched on the cliff-top, it can only be reached by a rather arduous climb up 800 steps rising in a series of hairpin bends. Those who prefer the discomfort and jolting of a Greek saddle to the exhausting climb on foot can ride up on a mule, which should in any case be used for carrying luggage. A visit to Santorin, often accomplished in a few hours, really requires two or three days, for the fascination of this island is a complex and constantly changing thing. From the village of Mavrogli, the highest point of the cliff, you should watch the sun sinking behind the island of Therasia whose volcanic mass assumes a variety of brown, grey and violet hues and, as night approaches, acquires a dark, resplendent glaze. A moonlight walk through the empty streets and among the mostly deserted houses of this village is a strangely unreal experience. Mavrogli was once the Catholic centre of the island, for Santorin at one time came under a strong French influence to which the convent and school of the Ursulines and the cathedral of Phira still bear witness; the presence of the Latin Church is a rare phenomenon in the Greek islands.

The excursion to ancient Thera will take a whole day if you avail yourself of the opportunity to have a bathe. If you are not a good walker you can go by taxi to Pyrgos, a pretty village which has also suffered much from earthquakes. From its high western cliff Santorin runs gently down to the sea in the east, its rich volcanic soil covered with vines and fields of tomatoes. Round a rocky ridge near Mount Haghios Ilias and its monastery lie the remains of Thera, colonized by the Dorians about the year

1000 BC, an active military city that founded Cyrene in Africa. The ruins – a gymnasium, baths and a theatre – date mostly from the Hellenistic and Roman periods. Santorin has two faces which one never forgets: the grand, fantastic and inhuman aspect of its rocky mass contrasting with the smiling grace of its rural life and the homely appeal of its little white villages.

Mykonos is the most dazzling of the Cyclades. Situated beside the sea, the town of Mykonos forms a sparkling white crescent. In the mid-day sun or in the moonlight you should climb up to the high ground where the famous windmills stand; from here you can observe the admirable geometrical layout of the town and the captivating interplay of forms and light. Mykonos is said to possess 365 chapels, donated by the island's leading families; the pyramid-shaped church of Paraportiani consists of five chapels of different volumes and levels. A stroll along the narrow streets of Mykonos offers all sorts of unexpected pleasures: mauve hibiscus on a white wall, or the green foliage of a mulberry-tree in a patio; on the outside staircases leading up to the first floor of each house, children play and old women knit; a donkey passes laden with two large baskets of melons and the vendor shouts *Ola ta sfazo!* ('I'll cut off the top'), so that the housewife can judge the melon's ripeness. Through the open doorways one can see the craftsmen at work and the women busying themselves with their domestic chores. The deliciously peaceful square of the Three Wells (Ta Tria Pigadia) is typical of this town which, devoid of all sophistication, radiates happiness and simplicity.

One of the important inhabitants of the island is Petros the pelican, who struts around the harbour. One day, the legend goes, when a flock of migrating pelicans was flying over the island, he landed in exhaustion on the beach near the town and then became its mascot. The sailors of Tinos, in

their jealousy, are supposed to have captured Petros at night and taken him back to their own island; the murky story of abduction ended in front of the court of Syra, which restored Petros to Mykonos. Whatever the life-span of a pelican might be, can this really be the same Petros who for the past thirty years has been greedily swallowing the fish he is offered and posing obligingly for photographers? There is nothing more like a pelican than another pelican – Petros will live for ever . . .

Mykonos has a great reputation. Twenty years ago I stayed there on several occasions, when it still depended on its own resources, honoured only by a few summer visitors. In those days one slept in the house of one of the local inhabitants, and in the warm-hearted friendliness of this little town one enjoyed simple pleasures, taking a boat every day to bathe on the beach of Haghios Stefanos and dancing in a taverna in the evening with the fishermen of the island; one could also listen to the splendid stories of Cambanis, a colourful character who would reinforce his eloquence with little glassfuls of cognac, and one frequented

the shop of the sweet and charming Sophia, who had some beautiful jewellery to offer the fashionable ladies from passing yachts. The memories of youth! I remember playing the part of Paris with three Athenian beauties, Teta, Iris and Roxana. One was a vivacious brunette, the second a rather touchy young woman with auburn hair and a mocking manner, and the third a blond girl with a very simple nature and a body of wonderful firmness.

On a short return visit to Mykonos recently I was appalled. It is now the Saint-Tropez of Greece, with hotels, shops and night-clubs and the same bizarre clientèle of bearded Scandinavians, American homosexuals, gazelle-like women and unwashed dandies – the noise and vulgarity of these pseudo-adventurers aping the life of luxury have invaded this paradise with a vengeance. Along the beaches on the south coast of the island, colonies of hippies go about naked in the sun of Apollo, taking drugs, making love, seeking the joys and liberties of paganism; but at least the pagan world displayed a creative energy and enthusiasm, a quality whose secret must be rediscovered if man is not to degrade

himself.

At first the islanders regarded these strangers with a dignified curiosity, naturally astonished by their way of life; but they have quickly become used to them, though not always approving of their excesses. The example of these young people who have come from all over the world, hungry for freedom and pleasure, has undoubtedly influenced the local boys and girls and imperilled the religious and family discipline that had been maintained on these islands for centuries. The same thing had already happened in other places: Capri and Saint-Tropez were once fishing villages, but today the grandchildren of the old fishermen work in restaurants, night-clubs and fashion boutiques. Admittedly, it can be claimed that Ulysses was the first hippy of the islands; but in certain parts of Greece the sudden transformation, which has taken place with the rapidity characteristic of the times, seems particularly brutal. As a spectator observing this irreversible trend one feels a certain nostalgia; one is inclined to think that these youngsters are dooming themselves to spurious pleasures and to pity them because of what they are going to lose – the ability to enjoy the simple life, something very precious and irreplaceable which is lacking in the world of today. Yet perhaps this is a romanticized nostalgia which ignores the poverty, the tedium and the misery of the life led by many of these people, who now can at least look to the future with hope.

Since these reflections might suggest that the author is an austere and even cantankerous person, I should like to show my appreciation of life's pleasures by quoting a passage from an enchanting poem by Theocritus entitled *Oaristys* (third century BC), which tells of a country girl who loses her virginity; the bawdy ballads of eighteenth-century France were to be inspired by this pastoral poem, but could not equal its particular flavour and freshness.

SHE

Hey! what are you doing, little satyr? You're putting your hand on my breasts!

HE

This is a first lesson for these apples of fine velvet.

SHE

I shall faint, lord Pan! Take your hand away quickly!

HE

Gently, now! Why are you trembling? How you are frightened my dear!

SHE

You throw me in the ditch and soil my fine clothes.

HE

No, I am putting a fur under you and your clothes.

SHE

But you're taking off my belt! Why have you untied it?

HE

It is the first present to give to Queen Paphos.

SHE

You wretch! Stop, there's someone coming. I think I hear a noise . . .

HE

It is the cypresses telling each other that you are marrying me.

SHE

But you've torn my shawl. Now I am quite naked . . .

HE

I shall give you other shawls and many pretty things.

SHE

You promise me gifts, but I shall not have a grain of salt.

. . . I came a virgin to these woods and I go home a woman.

From Mykonos it takes less than an hour by motor-boat to reach **Delos**, unless the *meltemi* is blowing too violently for a sea crossing.

O Delos! Dear Delos! Land of wind and toil, a rock beaten by the waves . . . Delos, planted in the sea, its shore washed by the foam of its waters,

in the words of the poet Callicrates. This denuded island, three miles long, round which the Cyclades, the Aegean Sea and the whole of Hellas seem to gravitate, was one of the most famous places of Antiquity. For a Greek, Delos was the scene of the birth of the divine twins, Apollo and

Artemis. Their mother Leto, one of the innumerable conquests of Zeus, was pursued by the vengeance of Hera and found refuge on this floating isle which Poseidon immobilized with a blow of his trident. In the Mycenaean period, however, Delos had known more ancient gods which the Apollonian triad, of Asian origin, did not replace until about the tenth century BC, at the time of the arrival of the Ionians who had fled from Attica and the Dorian invaders. The cult of four maidens believed to have come from the north, the Hyperborean Virgins, goddesses of fertility, survived for a long time; girls about to be married would offer them a wisp of their hair. By the seventh century BC Delos was the religious centre of the Ionian confederacy. In the sixth century it fell into the power of Pisistratus, tyrant of Athens, who decided to purify the sanctuary by ridding it of its tombs. After the Punic wars Delos became the seat of the first maritime league, organized and soon dominated by Athens. In 426 BC Athens promulgated a decree prohibiting births and deaths on the sacred island, which it regarded as the shrine of its ancestors; to invest it with a greater splendour the city instituted the first *Delia*, a religious festival celebrated every four years. In the third year of the Olympiads, in the month of May, the *Delias* or 'Delian ship' of Theseus left Piraeus laden with priests, singers, dancers and the oxen intended for slaughter. The Athenian ambassadors attended the festivals organized to celebrate the birth of Apollo and which were accompanied by the traditional rejoicings (sacrifices, processions, choruses, athletic contests and horse races). About 314 BC Delos regained its independence and under the patronage first of the Ptolemies of Egypt, then of the Macedonian dynasty, enjoyed

THE TERRACE OF THE LIONS

great prosperity. The arrival of the Italians at the beginning of the second century and the destruction of Corinth in 146 BC ensured its commercial supremacy throughout the Aegean; the island became the centre of trade between Asia, Greece and Italy. Even if, for a time, Rome remained in the shadow of Athens, it soon dominated Delos, driving out the native population and replacing it with hordes of bankers, shipowners and merchants from the Mediterranean world. Delos was the great emporium for oil, corn, wine, pottery and slaves. At the height of its activity and prosperity, having hitherto benefited from the sacred neutrality which it owed to its sanctuary, the city suffered a brutal death-blow: in 88 BC it was sacked and burnt by the admirals of Mithridates, king of Pontus and the bitter enemy of Rome; its Italian population was exterminated.

Thereafter Delos had only ruins to testify to its past glory. Owing to its dual religious and commercial vocation, this site presents the most varied assortment of ancient remains in Greece. Here one finds all the elements of the life of Antiquity: a great Pan-Hellenic sanctuary, the Temple of Apollo, with its associated cults, the temples of Artemis, Dionysus, Hera and of foreign divinities such as the Egyptian Serapis, Isis and Anubis, the Syrian Hadad and Atargatis (the orgiastic Astarte, who here seems to have become a more sober deity); on Mount Cynthus a sacred cave inhabited by underworld gods of more ancient origin; a Sacred Lake which is now dry but which Herodotus compared with that of Saïs in Egypt; a seaboard trading city with harbours, warehouses, agoras, a hypostyle building that served as an exchange for its merchants, and the numerous edifices of the merchants' associations, such as the Poseidoniasts of Berytus (Beirut); and, finally, the luxurious villas of the wealthy merchants in the theatre district, the House of Masks, the House of the Trident and the House of Dionysus, decorated with brilliant mosaics of wonderful inventive power.

The traveller, who usually lands at the Sacred Harbour, adjacent to the ancient trading port, will need a fertile imagination to bring to life this great expanse of ruins. These quays and warehouses were once crowded with sailors from all corners of the Mediterranean. In the Hypostyle Hall the names of the boats and the nature and weight of their cargoes were called out, and the shipowners and merchants conducted their business. The Agora of the Italians, occupying twenty-five acres, was the busiest district; here a noisy and motley crowd thronged under the colonnades and round the shops, buying fabrics and jewellery or, as offerings to the gods, peacocks, turtle-doves and beautiful stuffed geese from Egypt. The Sacred Lake is now reduced to dust, but in ancient times swans glided over its bright waters. The Temple of Apollo was visited by an endless procession of pilgrims.

O Delos! Land of altars, land of prayers, what sailor, what merchant of the Aegean would dare to sail past your coasts in his fast ship?

sang Callimachus.

The sanctuary had an oracle, which was eclipsed by that at Delphi; but, through his diligent priests, Apollo, the landlord of the island, exacted his tithe on all land transactions and commercial operations. His jars of gold, kept in the temple treasury, were the symbol of fabulous wealth. Among the ruins of the many different sanctuaries which are now razed to the ground, the only relic of the mighty glory of this god, who reigned for a thousand years over the privileged island, is a paltry bust, part of a colossal statue which the Venetians cut into pieces.

Nevertheless, some of the surviving monuments of this vast city, which had 25,000 inhabitants in the second century BC, are still astonishingly evocative. The famous Terrace of the Lions, for example; the lions, hewn from the marble of Naxos, were originally nine but are now only five in number; their bodies tensed, raised on their hindquarters, they still seem to roar. The Temple of Dionysus bears witness to the wholesome and joyous erotic atmosphere that once prevailed here; the stelae of the phallus-bird, the emblem of happiness and fertility carried in processions, are decorated with delightfully expressive bas-reliefs such as that of the young bride being carried to the marriage bed. The House of Inopus (named after the neighbouring river which flowed from Mount Cynthus into the Sacred Lake), with its two storeys, its kitchen and its bathrooms, hardly seems to have been deserted for thousands of years; in contrast to the 'shacks' of the Athenians, it suggests the comforts of a middle-class dwelling and foreshadows the great Roman villas.

However, the great adventure that Delos offers does not really lie in its past; it is to be found, rather, in the living reality of this place which, unlike Pompeii, is not merely a dead city but has preserved an eternal radiance. The view from the top of the theatre is superb: the narrow grey masses of the islands of Hecate and Rhenea, separated by the deep blue bands of the sea – all is movement and yet nothing changes.

Although the tourist pavilion has only a few rooms, you should spend the night at Delos to watch the sun setting on Mount Cynthus; no more than 150 metres high, the mountain then assumes an astounding aspect, a tragic dimension evocative of its cavern where the island's earliest gods had their domain. A moonlight walk is an unearthly experience, with toads croaking at the bottom of the ancient cisterns and fat lizards, perennial inhabitants of the island, crossing your path. But the most extraordinary moment is the rising of the sun above the summit of Mount Cynthus, a spectacle as stirring as the most sublime symphony. Slowly the islands of the Aegean assume their shapes and colours: Tinos to the north, Mykonos to the east, Syra, Zea and Kythnos to the west, Paros and Naxos to the south. Greece awakens . . .

By the time one has visited most of them the **Cyclades** gradually lose their individuality; the most vivid memories are of some humorous incident or interesting encounter. The fragrance and colouring of each island take their place in a geography of the heart, and only a skilful and scrupulous poet could express their diversity in words. **Ios** is green and beautiful, the sails of its mills still turning in the wind. **Siphnos**, rich in gold and silver in ancient times, is a delicious haven with its old houses and their wooden balconies; the village of Kastro, at the foot of a Venetian fortress, has a splendour unequalled in the Aegean. In the harbour of Kamares, in the evening, the population takes boat-trips. **Seriphos** is wild and rather melancholy. **Paros,** where rock and vine mingle, has nobility; its quarries, which provided the marble for countless masterpieces, are now disused. The inhabitants are very friendly and in the summer the island receives its regular visitors from Athens. **Naxos** is the

148

largest and most fertile of the Cyclades. Shortly after her departure from Crete, Ariadne was abandoned there by the ungrateful Theseus, but she soon found consolation in the arms of a handsome castaway, the god Dionysus.

The islands of Hydra, **Spetsai** and **Poros** lie along the north-east coast of the Peloponnesus, not far from Athens. Though now the haunts of artists, sophisticated people and hippy groups in their dirty garb, the towns have retained a rare elegance, the imprint of several centuries of Venetian occupation. The geometrically shaped houses of ochre, yellow, white, blue and pink which line the harbour and stand side by side on the hillside look like little Venetian palaces. Arriving in Poros is an unusual experience, for the harbour faces on to the town of Galata on the mainland and the boat seems to be sailing between the houses; behind their coloured cubes lie fields of lemons and olives.

Hydra played a vital part in the War of Independence; in fact, it is not an exaggeration to say that the defeat of the Turkish fleet was to a large extent the achievement of this little island, which then numbered 28,000 inhabitants. The courage and daring of its sailors and its celebrated captains, Miaoulis, Koundoriotis and Tombazis, proved decisive. These warrior virtues doubtless owed much to the presence of a large number of Albanian Orthodox refugees, who were bitter enemies of the Turks and had established themselves on Hydra in the sixteenth and seventeenth centuries. The fabulous wealth of the island's leading families made it possible to equip a formidable fleet. Their prosperity, dating from the eighteenth century, had been based on the cereal trade with southern Russia, the construction of merchant sailing-ships (*saktaria, latinadikta*) famous throughout the eastern Mediterranean, and piracy, an activity in which the people of Hydra had always excelled. The English admiral Codrington, who had sunk the Turkish squadron at Navarino, warned Capodistria, the head of the provisional Greek government, that he would turn his cannons against the Greek ships if the pirates continued to plunder merchant vessels. And so Hydra exchanged wealth for glory; its maritime activity declined rapidly, but it has retained its love of the sea and today its sons are sailing on all the oceans of the world. It was a Greek writer who said that Hydra produces sour pears, the best sea-captains and the least ineffectual heads of government. Once renowned for its innumerable springs and its pine-forests, the island is now denuded and has to import its water. The harbour, the pretty lanes of the town and the white-washed houses form a lovely scene. Thanks to the tourist trade and its hotels, Hydra has come back to life; once a heroic island, it now lives on its charm.

It is perhaps worth recalling that the mark left by Venice on the Greek islands has its origin in the agreement reached between the doge Dandolo and the leaders of the Fourth Crusade (1204). In return for transporting and supplying the 30,000 soldiers and the 5,000 horses of this expedition which was intended to liberate the Holy Places, but which found it more lucrative to set about the conquest of the Christian Empire of the East, Venice demanded the capture of Zara, in Dalmatia, which had rebelled against her, and the assignment to her government of half of all the conquests made by this strange crusade. Although the Latin Empire of the West lasted only fifty years – Michael Palaeologus recaptured Constantinople in 1261 – Venice was to rule over the islands and coasts of Greece and Dalmatia for much longer, until she was driven out by the Turks in the sixteenth and seventeenth centuries.

The most Venetian of the Greek islands is, appropriately, **Corfu**; well protected by its fortifications, the island repulsed the assaults of the Ottoman fleet and remained under

151

the rule of the Serene Republic until the end of the eighteenth century. The ancient Kerkyra, a colony founded in the eighth century BC by Corinth on the route to Sicily, was annexed to the Empire of the East in AD 336. It owes to Byzantium its name of Stous Korphous, 'the town of the peaks', no doubt signifying the high summits of Mount Pantocrator, in the north of the island, with its almost inaccessible little churches and monasteries. In 1387 Corfu appealed to Venice to protect it against the Berbers from North Africa and remained under Venetian tutelage until 1797. The presence of the French armies, victorious throughout Europe, was to leave its mark in Esplanade Square with its fine arcaded houses. During their unpopular occupation of 1816–64 the British built the royal palace, developed irrigation, blew up most of the Venetian fortifications (but luckily not the old fortress) and introduced cricket, which is still popular and is known as *to gamé* ('the game').

Corfu is called the 'Garden of Ionia'. (It should be pointed out that the term 'Ionia' can lead to geographical confusion, since the Ionian coast is in fact the coast of Asia Minor where the Ionians took refuge around the eighth century BC, after being driven from Greece by the Dorian conquest.) Corfu provides a striking contrast to the naked barrenness of many Greek islands, some of which were once places of greenery but have been totally stripped of trees and ravaged by herds of goats. Its olives, oranges and lemons are renowned for their quality. Strawberries are cultivated in large quantities, as is garlic, of which the islanders make much use. Roses, marguerites and clematis grow wild – is this, perhaps, by favour of St Spiridon, the island's patron-saint, little known in the liturgy but whose name is constantly invoked in Corfu and whose feast is celebrated with much splendour? The town of Corfu, with its mixture of styles, has an old-fashioned charm reminiscent not so much of Venice as of certain lakeside towns in northern Italy, such as Como or Lugano. The Georgian royal palace now accommodates the archaeological museum, which possesses one of the masterpieces of Archaic art: the pediment of the Temple of Artemis (sixth century BC), decorated with an enormous Gorgon girdled with serpents and who sticks out her tongue as she tramples on her enemies. The site of the ancient Corcyra, however, which is adjacent to the modern town, is quite lacking in atmosphere.

Corfu has long been a major tourist resort and its modernized amenities now offer a wide variety of choice. Two excursions are not to be missed. The first is to the nearby terrace of Kanoni, the site of an old Venetian cannon, which offers an entrancing view of the islet on which the eighteenth-century monastery of Vlachernae stands; the island is joined to Corfu by a long causeway. Further away, the isle of Pondikonisi was supposed to have

been the ship in which the Phaeacians were bringing Ulysses back to Ithaca and which Poseidon, in his fury, transformed into stone as Ulysses was approaching the island. If you go on to Benitses you will see, in a perfect setting of delightful gardens, the large Neo-Classical villa built in 1890 at the request of the empress Elizabeth of Austria, the lonely and capricious wife of Francis Joseph. On her death the Achilleion was bought by the emperor of Germany, Wilhelm II, who stayed there on many occasions before 1914. Decorated with frescoes of questionable taste, this grandiose edifice has now been turned into a casino.

The other recommended excursion is to Paleo Kastritsa, on the west coast about twenty kilometres from the town. A monastery stands on a promontory overlooking the sea, and on the terrace of the neighbouring peninsula the French scholar Victor Bérard located the capital of Alcinous, king of the Phaeacians and father of Nausicaa.

This beautiful spot is certainly worthy of Homer. The beach on the neighbouring bay of Ermones is supposed to be the place where the king's daughter and her servants, who had come to wash their linen, discovered the divine castaway, the naked Ulysses, while playing ball. Here is the ideal spot for reading that wonderfully simple passage in the *Odyssey* where the young girl and the wily warrior fall immediately in love, a love which was never to be declared and which illumines some pages of sublime poetry. 'Nausicaa with the white arms', 'Nausicaa with the proud heart', is not a heroine but the ideal Greek maiden:

And the mules were trotting or stepping high.
And so that Ulysses and the servants could follow them on foot,
The maiden who was driving barely used the whip . . .

On every island the liveliest place is always the harbour, and one never tires of its bustle of activity. Fishermen mend the meshes of their yellow nets, using both hands and feet, while a child softens an octopus by beating it against the stone of the quay (the tentacles, fried and sprinkled with oil, are delicious to eat). Some of the boats, which are brightly coloured in red, green and blue, are fitted with acetylene lamps, for they go out at night fishing for spiny lobster; others bring back gilt-heads and especially red mullet, which is here the fish with the most delicate flesh. But the lord of the Greek waters is the dolphin, which the Ancients regarded as an incarnation of Apollo. This marine mammal, about six feet long, is exceptionally intelligent and has a capricious, playful nature; it loves to show off and can be seen following in the wake of a boat and swimming without effort, drawn along by the back-wash, or choosing a big wave blown up by the *meltemi* and letting itself be swept along, indulging in its own variety of surf-riding; it also performs leaps and somersaults, and its delightful frolics seem to be inviting the spectator to share its freedom and happiness.

To paraphrase Sophocles, one might say that there are many wonders in Greece, but that none is more wonderful than the Greeks themselves. Henry Miller has described them as 'like men ought to be – that is to say, open, frank, natural, spontaneous, warm-hearted'. It is true, the Greeks have an innate sense of human comradeship and their joy in life is so intense that it radiates around them; in their company one rediscovers the freshness and the freedom of childhood and forgets the vanities and false airs which humanity commonly assumes. Here lies the true Greek miracle, a quality that belongs to the simplest people – sailors, peasants and craftsmen. In Greece, however, one can also be offended by the vulgarity and the bad taste of those who move in the world of business. In Greek 'society', which has hardly any roots in the past, one often finds an irritating snobbery. The more genuinely cultured Greeks, of whom there are many, do not parade themselves. For

years I have travelled in Greece for my own pleasure, and at one time I also happened to work there in a professional capacity – a disillusioning experience, for venality and bad faith were sometimes concealed by the most obliging manners. I have unhappy memories of a certain Basil, with his close-set eyes and his deceitful contracts, and of Mario, our director, who was like a fat pasha and seemed to consider himself entitled to extract his percentage from everybody and everything. This abuse of position and privilege has long been one of the most unpleasant aspects of Greek social life. Fortunately, there is an increasingly large number of dynamic and enterprising men for whom business is a fascinating and honourable game – but how could anyone hope to equal the skill and imagination of the Cephalonian who today, by his own merit, is the head of the leading tourist organization in Greece?

To close this book I should like to recall a few friendly faces. Nikko, for instance, who lives on his boat, sombre and reserved, but who suddenly gives you his friendship with a look; he conducts lucky tourists round the islands, and one could travel to the ends of the earth with him, for he has the virtues of discretion and of always being at hand when needed. One day, as Nikko and I have been promising each other for years, we shall set off together to hunt boar in Macedonia or to shoot the pigeons that nest in the caves of Cythera.

The impeccable Albert, his white mane well oiled and holding his short frame erect, has the air of a Neapolitan Don Juan; nearly eighty years old, he still swaggers every time a pretty woman passes, without appearing ridiculous – which is no mean feat! Beneath this high-spirited exterior lies a concern for things of the heart; and, if he likes to make his little profits and is susceptible to flattery, he is not alone; what is more, he loves France like his own mother, and since France has forgotten to give him the little red ribbon of the Legion of Honour which he cherishes so fondly, I award him the finest medal of all – the medal for enjoying life.

When we used to travel together in Greece, Yannis knew only two words of French, two short words which he always used in the interrogative: '*beau?*' and '*bon?*' I knew about five words in Greek: *kalo* ('all right'), *effkaristo poli* ('thank you very much'), *kalimera* ('good-morning, good-afternoon'), *krassi* ('wine') and *yasou* ('to your health'); but we spent some fascinating days together. Yannis was then a taxi-driver and now owns a little fleet of cars and coaches – well done, Yannis! We were always stopping somewhere, for he would insist that I taste a scented cheese, some delicious olives, or some plums in brandy renowned throughout the Peloponnesus. Yannis looked after me like a mother-hen, choosing the leanest piece of lamb, the firmest mullet or the lightest *retsina*. If today I can claim to know a little about Greece, it is because I have eaten its food and because the taste is still in my mouth.

Nowadays, when someone else is always blamed for one's own unhappiness or misfortune, it is to the great credit of the Greek people that they still accept their responsibilities. They can face adversity, and they can also create the simple joys that are the sweetness of life. Happiness is an attitude of the heart; to persuade ourselves of this fact, let us leave the final words to a peasant who could well be a Greek of today, though the words he speaks were written twenty-five centuries ago. After a hard day's work, as the rain is beginning to fall, he is organizing his little banquet:

'Is there anything more pleasant than to see the land sown and, while a god waters it, to say to one's neighbour: Hey! Comarchides! what should we do now? Should we drink together since the gods are with us? Come, wife, roast three plates of beans, mix them with some grains of wheat and serve us some figs . . . and bring a thrush and two finches . . . and also some whey and four pieces of hare . . . Ask Eschinades for some myrtle branches with berries, and on the way shout to Charinadis to come and drink a glass with us.'

The origins of Greece and the Archaic period

(second millennium – sixth century BC)

● The early Greeks, who were of Indo-European origin, occupied the peninsula at the beginning of the second millennium. Contact between these invaders and the Cretan civilization (seventeenth–sixteenth centuries) resulted in the Mycenaean civilization which reached its zenith in the fifteenth to thirteenth centuries. But around 1100 BC a new wave of Indo-European conquerors, the Dorians, began to submerge Hellas. The Mycenaean world crumbled and civilization suffered a set-back – from the twelfth to ninth centuries Greece passed through a dark age. The old Ionian and Aeolian populations were pushed towards the islands and the coast of Asia Minor.

● Greek civilization proper began in the eighth century BC. During the Archaic period it enjoyed a rapid development aided by trading contacts with the East. The governments of the cities evolved in roughly the same manner. The monarchy of early times was progressively limited by the prerogatives of the aristocracy, which in its turn assumed power. In the seventh century the introduction of coinage modified the framework of society; craft activity and commerce were stimulated and social conditions transformed.

● At the end of the seventh century an acute social crisis led to rule by tyrants who, with the support of the people and the new middle class, drove out the aristocrats. The aristocracy was often to return to power, but henceforth governed in a more liberal fashion. Throughout the sixth century, while the aristocratic and warlike Sparta stagnated in immobility, Athens made swift progress towards democracy. Solon devised its first democratic Constitution (594), which Pisistratus and his sons abolished (561–510), but Clisthenes restored it in a more liberal form (507). At the end of the eighth century the Greeks had launched their conquest of the Mediterranean basin and founded colonies in southern Italy and Sicily and in Asia Minor. This expansion proved beneficial to the economic and demographic stability of the mother-cities; the colonies, whilst politically independent, still maintained these economic and religious bonds.

Classical, Hellenistic and Roman Greece

(fifth century BC – fourth century AD)

● After Athens had supported the Greek cities of Asia Minor against the Persian conquest, Darius launched an expedition against Greece. In 490 his troops were repulsed by the Athenians at Marathon. Ten years later, Xerxes attempted another invasion, but his fleet was routed at Salamis (480) and his soldiers defeated at Plataea (479). The end of the Persian wars marked the beginning of the political apogee of Athenian democracy. The cities of Greece combined in the confederacy of Delos under the authority of Athens (478). Soon this free association of cities had been transformed into the Athenian empire. The 'century of Pericles' (470–429) saw the political, economic, intellectual and artistic supremacy of Athens.

An Outline of Greek History

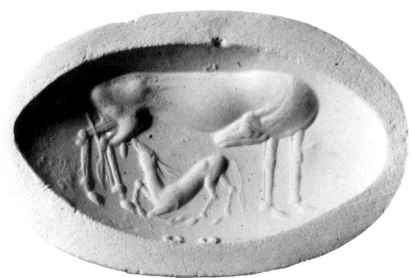

● The prosperity of Athens did not survive the Peloponnesian War, in which the city engaged in conflict with Sparta (431–404). The death of Pericles (429), the imprudence of Alcibiades and then his treachery at the time of the disastrous Sicilian expedition (415–413) led to the decline of Athens; its fleet was defeated at Aigospotami (405). Lysander, commander-in-chief of Sparta, occupied the city and demolished the Long Walls of Piraeus. By the end of the fifth century Sparta had established its hegemony over all Greece. But the Spartan army was beaten at Leuctra (371) by the Theban forces whose leaders, Pelopidas and Epaminondas, assured the supremacy of their city for some twenty years. In 359 the advent of Philip of Macedon profoundly modified the balance of power in the Greek world; he captured Amphipolis (357) and Potidaea (356) and razed Olynthus (348). At the urging of Demosthenes, Athens at last recognized the danger

Impressions of Cretan seals (15th century BC)

and made an alliance with Thebes. Philip crushed the armies of the two cities at Chaeronea (338), thereby making himself master of the whole of Greece. He was assassinated in 336. His son Alexander succeeded him and embarked on the conquest of Asia (336–323). On his death in 323 Alexander's empire extended from Egypt to India.

● Alexander's generals divided the empire among themselves, but in 214 BC the rivalries among their successors resulted in the first Roman intervention. The two wars in which the Romans fought against the dynasty of the Antigonidae ended with the defeat of the Macedonian commander Perseus (197). But Greece was still free. After another military intervention by the Roman general Aemilius Paulus who was victorious at Pydna (168), the kingdom of Macedonia was brought under the authority of Rome. The rest of Greece tried to resist Roman domination; Corinth was razed in 146. In the reign of Augustus (31 BC to AD 14) Greece became a Roman province under the name of Achaia. In the second century AD the emperor Hadrian's passion for Hellenism set an official seal on the influence exercised by Greece on the civilization of Rome. Athens remained an intellectual capital, but no longer played a major political or economic role.

● The Barbarians ravaged Greece on several occasions during the third century. In the reign of Constantine (AD 324–37) Christianity became the state religion; the decline of Greece was accelerated as the emperors waged their campaign against Hellenic thought and religion. In the reign of Theodosius I the Olympic Games were celebrated for the last time, in 393. In 395 the Goths again devastated Greece. On the death of Theodosius the division of the Roman Empire gave Greece to the Empire of the East.

Byzantine and Turkish domination
(395–1832)

● The Byzantines had to defend Greece against the invasions of the Huns, the Slavs (eighth–ninth centuries) and then the Bulgars. The Fourth Crusade of 1204 never reached its destination, the Holy Land, but ended with the capture of Byzantium. Greece was then divided between the victors, Venice and the Frankish princes. The merchants of Venice chose the islands and the ports, while the Franks built the citadels that were to protect their counties, the Morea (Peloponnesus), the duchy of Athens, the depostat of Epirus and the kingdom of Salonica. In 1261, however, Michael Palaeologus recaptured Constantinople and thereafter the Byzantines gradually reconquered their former territories, except for the islands, which remained under the rule of Venice.

● The seizure of Byzantium by the Turks (1453) put an end to the Empire of the East, which had existed for eleven centuries. The Greek influence, decisive in the Byzantine period, was still evident under the Ottoman Empire. In 1458–60 the Turks occupied the duchy of Athens. Their expansion was halted by the Treaty of Karlowitz (1699) which left the Peloponnesus to the Venetians. In the sixteenth and seventeenth centuries a large number of Orthodox Albanians of the emirate of Janina emigrated to Greece and were subsequently to play an important part in her history.

● In the seventeenth century, as the Turkish domination became more oppressive, resistance was organized both within and outside Greece. A national consciousness began to take shape, especially after the Turks had completed their conquest with the capture of the Peloponnesus (1715). In 1815 Ypsilanti founded the Society of Friends in Odessa, and at this same time the philhellenic movement was spreading through Europe.

● In 1821 the Greek insurrection and the intervention of the European Great Powers (Russia, Britain and France) threatened the Ottoman occupation. After the victory of Navarino (1827) and the second Treaty of London (1830), Greece obtained independence under the protection of the three Powers. A modest state of 600,000 inhabitants, Greece became a monarchy under Otto of Bavaria. In 1832 the Sublime Porte recognized Greek independence.

From independence to modern Greece

● The new kingdom had as its capital first Nauplia, then Athens (1833). It comprised only the Peloponnesus, the Cyclades and a part of the Greek mainland, and was still heavily dependent on foreigners. In 1843 Otto had to renounce authoritarian monarchy and grant a Constitution. Insurrection broke out again at Nauplia in 1862, the Bavarian dynasty was deposed and Otto replaced by a provisional government. The following year Britain found a new ling, George I, from Denmark. The Russo-Turkish War (1877–8) resulted in the enlargement of the Greek state.

● The military league which made a successful *coup* in 1909 called on a young Cretan, Eleutherios Venizelos. Appointed prime minister, Venizelos exercised skilful diplomacy in the Balkans which resulted in the Balkan agreement of 1912 (Greece, Serbia and Bulgaria). A liberal state was created by the Constitution of 1911. After George I had been assassinated at Salonica (1913), his son Constantine pursued a pro-German policy. Venizelos overthrew him in 1917 and until the end of the Great War the fate of Greece was linked with that of France and the Allies.

● In 1921–2 the Greco-Turkish War erupted in Asia Minor, ending with massive exchanges of population. George II had to abdicate in 1923; the republic lasted only twelve years and in 1936, with the dictatorship of Metaxas, the monarchy was restored.

● During the Second World War the political forces of Greece united to resist first the Italians and then the Germans. The Dodecanese islands were annexed to Greece in 1947. But, with peace, the old political discord reappeared and a cruel civil war divided the country. The constitutional monarchy remained, precariously. In 1967 a junta of colonels seized power and established an authoritarian government. In June 1973 the monarchy was abolished and a republic proclaimed; in the following November the Papadopoulos régime was overthrown by another military *coup*.

Greek coins (6th and 5th century BC)

LITERATURE

AESCHYLUS

The earliest of the Greek tragedians of the Classical age, Aeschylus was born in 525 BC. He fought at Marathon and at Salamis, and died in 456. Only seven of his ninety tragedies have survived, including *The Persians*, the *Oresteia* trilogy, *Seven against Thebes* and *Prometheus Bound*. Writing about problems that touched the hearts of his audiences, he enjoyed immense popularity. A deeply religious person, he urged men to bow to the will of the gods. The nobility of his inspiration, the power of his creative imagination and his unerring sense of the dramatic made him one of the very greatest tragic poets of Greece.

ARISTOPHANES

Aristophanes was born in Athens about 445 BC and died around 380. Of the forty-four comedies he wrote, only eleven have survived; studded with scintillating humour, they provide a vivid picture of Athenian society in the Classical period, for Aristophanes drew the comedy of his situations from the political and social life of the time. He satirized the venality of the law courts (*The Wasps*), Socrates and the philosophers (*The Clouds*), and various absurd legends (*The Frogs*). He was the father of Classical satirical comedy and his comic genius was unequalled in the ancient world.

DEMOSTHENES

Demosthenes was born in Athens in 384 BC and at an early age began to discipline himself in the art of oratory. A man of energy and will-power, he strove all his life to assert his personality. He made speeches remarkable for their rigorous reasoning and nobility of language. From 351 onwards he fiercely opposed Philip of Macedon, denouncing his political ambition (IV *Philippics* and III *Olynthiacs*). He also attacked his political enemies, but was condemned to exile and had to take poison at Calauria (322) to escape the Macedonians. The

EURIPIDES

The youngest of the great Greek tragedians of the Classical age, Euripides lived from 480 to 406 BC. He was a pupil of the sophists and wrote ninety-two plays of which seventeen are extant, including *Medea*, *Hippolytus* and *Andromache*. He won only four prizes and was little appreciated during his lifetime. Written during the Golden Age of Athens, his works reveal a critical spirit which questioned the traditional order, expressing man's profound dissatisfaction with his human condition and destiny. His characters were subsequently to enjoy an extraordinary literary history.

HERODOTUS

Born in Asia Minor, Herodotus lived from about 485 to 425 BC. He travelled much in Egypt and Persia, and spent a long time in Athens. Although the Persian wars form the subject of his *History*, they serve as a pretext for detailed descriptions of the different regions of the Persian Empire and the customs of their populations. Herodotus was equally meticulous in recording the extraordinary stories that he had heard and his work can thus be accused of lacking in critical sense. Yet the charm of these exotic tales, the clarity of the narrative in spite of frequent digressions, and his curiosity and impartiality make him a delightful story-teller.

HESIOD

Born in Boeotia in the second half of the eighth century BC, Hesiod was the earliest of the Greek poets after Homer. He was deprived of his inheritance by his brother Perses, who ruined himself and then came to him for help. Hesiod replied to his brother with sound practical advice in the *Works and Days*, a poem devoted to agriculture. The *Theogony* lists genealogies of gods and is an invaluable source of information concerning the mythology of the Archaic period. The Greeks regarded

Famous Greeks of Antiquity

Details of pottery
Soldier (hoplite) leaving for war
Achilles and Ajax playing dice
Hercules

Hesiod as one of their greatest poets; children studied his works at school, together with those of Homer. Unfortunately, in translation his poetry loses a great deal and makes rather tedious reading.

HOMER

It seems that Homer lived in the first half of the eighth century BC, possibly at Smyrna and Cos, but nothing can be stated with certainty concerning his life. In Antiquity he was revered as the author of the *Iliad* (the epic of the siege of Troy) and the *Odyssey* (the adventures of Ulysses on his way home from Troy). In these two poems Homer paints a picture of the Mycenaean civilization of four hundred years earlier, as well as of the Archaic civilization of which he was a contemporary. His genius asserts itself in the composition of both poems, in the realism and beauty of the descriptions, the depiction of the characters and the splendour of the imagery. A knowledge of his work was clearly the basis of Hellenic culture.

PINDAR

Pindar, who was born near Thebes in 518 BC, belonged to the Boetian aristocracy. Like Aeschylus, his contemporary, he had a deeply religious nature. He excelled in all the lyrical genres and wrote both religious (*Paeans, Dithyrambs*) and secular poems. The four books of the *Epinicia* or *Triumphal Odes* celebrate the victories of the athletes at the Olympic, Pythian, Isthmian and Nemean games and, in particular, the victor's family, his country and the gods who made his success possible. He died in 438. Pindar's poetry is full of grandeur and brilliance; he was the last great exponent of choral verse.

SOPHOCLES

Sophocles was born near Athens in 496 BC and died at the age of ninety. An extremely prolific writer endowed with a powerful personality, he also distinguished himself as a politician, a military chief and an athlete. He is said to have written a hundred and twenty-three plays which earned him numerous prizes. The most famous are those that recount the legends of Oedipus and Elektra (*Oedipus Rex,*

Antigone, Elektra, Oedipus at Colonus). Sophocles gives life and individuality to his characters, emphasising the pathos of their situations with a sober lyricism. His dramas bear the grave but noble imprint of Classicism.

THUCYDIDES

Thucydides belonged to an aristocratic Athenian family and owned gold-mines in Thrace. He was *strategos* in 424 BC; accused of failing to prevent the capture of Amphipolis by the Spartans, he was exiled for twenty years during which time he wrote his *History of the Peloponnesian War*. More is known about these twenty years than about any other period of Antiquity. Thucydides' information is comprehensive, clear and precise. He wanted to create a truly scientific history whose aims he explained at the beginning of his work. His fondness for analysis and his objectivity did not prevent him from expressing his indignation at events that shocked his national consciousness. His qualities as an historian were reinforced by a strong personality that made his writings particularly vivid.

XENOPHON

Xenophon lived from about 427 to 355 BC. He followed the teachings of the sophists and then of Socrates. His work consists principally of two historical studies, the *Anabasis* (an account of the expedition of 401 in which he took part with 10,000 Greek mercenaries in the service of Cyrus, king of Persia), the *Hellenica* (a continuation of the *History* of Thucydides, from 411 to 362) and the *Memorabilia*, a record of his memories of Socrates. Xenophon's thought and style are clear but lack any distinctive quality; his historical works, however, are a source of interesting information.

PHILOSOPHY AND SCIENCE

ARISTOTLE

Aristotle (384–322 BC), together with Plato, dominated philosophical thought in the fourth century. He was the tutor of Alexander and founded a school

of philosophy, the Lyceum, at Athens. Contrary to Plato, he considered that the philosopher should seek an explanation of the universe by starting from a vast collection of known facts. With his disciples he therefore embarked on an encyclopaedic series of writings in which, with the exception of mathematics, he displayed his competence in all the branches of knowledge.

DEMOCRITUS

Democritus of Abdera (*c.* 460–370 BC) was the heir to the philosophical tradition of Ionia. He believed that the world was composed of invisible and indestructible particles and of empty space, and that the movement and combination of these complementary atoms had created the universe.

HERACLITUS

Heraclitus of Ephesus (*c.* 576–480 BC) was an Ionian philosopher of the sixth century. He regarded fire as the primary element of the universe and thought that the conflict of contrary principles produced the harmony of the universe, which was in a perpetual state of flux.

PLATO

Born in 429 BC, Plato was the disciple and friend of Socrates. It was his ambition to mould the men who, after a long apprenticeship, would govern Athens. This education would direct the soul towards the knowledge and contemplation of the Good and the True, which the philosopher was able to perceive beyond outward appearances. Plato founded a school, the Academy, where he taught his numerous disciples. His work consists of philosophical dialogues, among them the *Apologia of Socrates,* the *Gorgias,* the *Republic* and the *Symposium.* He died in 347, having left a profound mark on Western philosophy.

PYTHAGORAS

Banished from Samos in the sixth century BC, Pythagoras took refuge in Crotona where he founded a school of philosophy that was more in the nature of a religious sect. The school combined two purposes: a scientific study which aimed to discover arithmetical relations in the universe, and an intense cultivation of moral perfection based on austere principles (stoïcism). The philosophy of Pythagoras exerted a strong influence during the Roman Empire.

SOCRATES

The son of a stone-cutter and a midwife, Socrates was born in Athens in 470 BC. He devoted himself to philosophy and had many disciples. He strove to perfect individual consciousness ('Know yourself') and guided his interlocutors to truth by asking them a succession of questions, often full of irony. Incurring the hostility of the representatives of the people and of the sophists, he was accused of having

Ephebe with basket

opposed the religion of the state and of having corrupted the youth. He refused to renounce any part of his teachings and was condemned to death. He drank hemlock after having declined to escape out of respect for the laws of Athens (399).

THALES

In the late seventh and early sixth centuries BC, Thales was one of the positivist philosophers of the school of Miletus. He believed water to be the origin of all things. By applying logical reasoning to the knowledge of the Babylonians he contributed to the progress of geometry, arithmetic and astronomy.

Hera and Prometheus

ARTS

LYSIPPUS

Lysippus was born at Sicyon at the beginning of the fourth century BC. His works were numerous, for he was an unusually prolific artist and remained active until the end of the fourth century. He continued the theoretical studies of Polycletus and carved athletes (*Apoxyomenos*), gods and allegories (*Kairos* or 'Opportunity', a copy of which is in Naples). His bronzes conveyed to perfection the movement of bodies and the facial expressions. The museum in Naples possesses several of his many works. He was the favourite sculptor of Alexander the Great.

MYRON

Like Phidias and Polycletus, Myron was the pupil of Hageladas of Argos, around the middle of the fifth century. His aim was to render movement, mainly in bronze. Only two of his works are known through copies: the *Athena and Marsyas* from the Acropolis (450–440) and the famous *Discobulus* (in the Museo Nazionale delle Terme in Rome).

PHIDIAS

Not much is known of the life of Phidias. A pupil of Hageladas of Argos, he probably began working as a sculptor after the Persian wars. His friend Pericles entrusted him with the supervision of the decoration of the Acropolis and of the Parthenon. Among his most famous works are the *Athena Promachos,* a bronze eight metres high which stood on the Acropolis (*c.* 453), and the gold and ivory statues of Zeus (for the temple at Olympia; *c.* 448) and of Athena (for the Parthenon; *c.* 438). The date of his death is not known. Regarded by the Greeks as the greatest of sculptors, he trained numerous pupils and exerted a widespread influence.

POLYCLETUS

A native of Argos, Polycletus was also the pupil of Hageladas. He made a gold and ivory statue for the Temple of Hera near Argos. His two masterpieces are the *Diadumenus* (an athlete crowning himself, now in the National Museum in Athens) and the *Doryphorus* (a lance-bearer, a marble copy of which is kept in Naples), which illustrated the system of proportions of the human body which Polycletus had expounded in his theoretical work the *Canon.* His statues were criticized for lacking an inner life, but Lysippus said that the *Doryphorus* was his only teacher, and the majority of the sculptors of Antiquity owed much to him.

PRAXITELES

The son of the sculptor Cephisodotus, Praxiteles lived in the fourth century BC, mainly at Athens. His mistress was the courtesan Phryné. The only extant sculpture which appears to be an original is the *Hermes Dionysophorus* found at Olympia. There are also some good ancient copies of his *Aphrodite of Cnidus* and *Apollo Sauroktonos* ('lizard-killer'). The distinguishing features of this artist who was universally admired in Antiquity are his religious inspiration and a gracefulness sometimes lacking in vigour.

SCOPAS

A native of Paros, Scopas worked in the middle of the fourth century BC on the decoration of the mausoleum at Halicarnassus (fragments in the British Museum), carved a historiated column of the Artemision at Ephesus and prepared the plans for the temple at Tegea. His statuary expresses both violence (*Maenad,* in the Dresden museum) and languor (*Pothos,* an allegory of Desire). His influence on Hellenistic art was considerable.

POLITICS

ALCIBIADES

Alcibiades was born *circa* 450 BC. He was the ward of Pericles and the disciple and friend of Socrates. An aristocrat by birth and in his tastes, of appealing intelligence and beauty, but conceited and unscrupulous, he scandalized his fellow-countrymen by his fondness for high living. He played a major role in politics. *Strategos* in 417, he proposed the Sicilian expedition which was entrusted to his command in 415. Accused of impious deeds and sentenced to death in his absence, he fled to Sparta and betrayed his country. Returning in triumph in 407, he was forced to go into exile once again, and was assassinated by the Thirty Tyrants in 404.

ALEXANDER THE GREAT

The son of Philip II of Macedon and his wife Olympias, Alexander was born at Pella in 356 BC. His tutor was Aristotle. He revealed his abilities as a strategist and his courage by defeating the coalition of Athens and Thebes at Chaeronea in 338. Becoming king on the death of his father, he embarked on the conquest of the Persian Empire. A first victory on the banks of the Granicus (334) gave him access to the western region of Asia Minor. To force the hand of destiny he cut the Gordian knot which, according to the oracle, he had to untie in order to become master of Asia. He achieved his goal by the victory at Issus (333), the capture of Tyre, the conquest of Egypt, the victory at Arbela (331) and the capture of Babylon, Susa and Persepolis. In 327 this triumphant expedition took him into western India. It was his ambition to bring about the political, religious and ethnic unity of the peoples of his empire; he married a Persian girl and 10,000 of his soldiers followed his example. He died at the age of 33, whilst he was dreaming of conquering western Europe. Appropriately, in view of his dual ancestry, his personality combined Greek prudence with Barbarian extravagance; he even dared to put himself on a footing with the gods. His empire did not survive him, but he had radically transformed the ancient world.

CLISTHENES

Grandson of the tyrant of Sicyon, Clisthenes led the defence of Athenian democracy against the aristocrats supported by Sparta, after the fall of the sons of Pisistratus. In 508–507 he restored the Constitution of Solon, making it more liberal and thus giving Athenian democracy a more durable framework.

EPAMINONDAS

Epaminondas was born of a noble but impoverished Theban family. As commander of the Theban army he liberated his city from Spartan domination in 379 BC. He collaborated in the reform of institutions and of the armed forces. Leading the 'sacred battalion' with his friend Pelopidas at Leuctra, he finally put an end to Spartan hegemony (371). Sharing the military and civil commands, Pelopidas and Epaminondas assured the power of Thebes until the arrival in Greece of Philip of Macedon.

PERICLES

Pericles was born around 495 BC, his mother belonging to the family of the Alcmaeonidae. Re-elected *strategos* each year, he directed the policies of Athens from 443 to 430. At first he used his influence to ensure the success of Athens in a series of wars against the Persians, Corinth, Aegina, Thebes and Sparta. The exploitation of the Athenian empire provided the resources necessary for his policy of large-scale building projects and artistic monuments, which included the Acropolis. His mistress, the beautiful Aspasia, made their house a meeting-place for artists, poets and philosophers. The Athenians held him responsible for the early failures in the Peloponnesian War and did not re-elect him as *strategos* in 430. They restored him to office the following year, but Pericles died in the great plague which ravaged the city (429).

PHILIP II OF MACEDON

Coming to power as regent at the age of 23, Philip II ousted his nephew from the throne and put himself at the head of a precarious kingdom. Soon, by cunning and violence, he succeeded in reunifying Macedonia and made it a powerful state. First he safeguarded the outlets to the sea by seizing Amphipolis (357) and Potidaea (356). Turning his attention to Greece, he razed Olynthus in 348 and was able to win a number of Greeks to his cause, including Isocrates and Aeschines. War broke out in 340. Philip captured Elatea in 339 and Chaeronea in 338, thereby crushing the Athenians and their allies. He then became the master of Greece and was preparing to attack the Persian Empire when he was assassinated in 336. He was succeeded by his son, Alexander the Great.

PISISTRATUS

Born of a noble family in Athens in the early sixth century, Pisistratus was the leader of a popular party. He seized power and became tyrant of Athens in 560. Twice driven from the city by the aristocrats, he re-established his tyranny around 540. He died in 527. Pisistratus encouraged the arts and literature, and undertook major building projects; he was succeeded by his two sons, Hippias and Hipparchus.

SOLON

Solon was born of a noble Athenian family about 640 BC. Elected *archon* for 594–593, he reformed the Constitution of Athens by finally breaking the hold which the powerful families had exercised over the citizens (social classes were redistributed and the assemblies modified). He improved the lot of the peasants and citizens by cancelling existing mortgages and abolishing enslavement for debt. He died in 559, after failing in his attempt to resist the tyrant Pisistratus.

THEMISTOCLES

Themistocles was born in Athens about 525 BC and became *archon* in 493. Political leader of the city from 490 to 480, he created the Athenian naval power by having triremes built and the harbours of Piraeus equipped. At the time of the second Persian invasion he ordered the Greek fleet to give battle at Salamis (480) and began the construction of the Long Walls. Banished from Athens by the aristocratic party, he died at the court of the king of Persia in 459.

Hercules fighting the Erymanthian boar

Legendary Gods and Heroes

Greek mythology began to take shape during the Mycenaean period (1580–1100 BC), when a synthesis of the religions of the Hellenes, of the earlier peoples and of the Cretans evolved, which was based on a feminine principle of fecundity, the mother-goddess. Both literature and art were deeply permeated with these myths, which have survived in the works of Homer and in Hesiod's *Theogony*. From their origins to the Hellenistic period, the images of divinity were gradually modified; the gods became more humanized and at the same time mystical beliefs appeared which promised a life beyond the grave. The deities of each city, such as Athena, were made the object of an official cult. The people remained deeply devoted to the divinities of nature (Demeter-Corē, for instance).

APOLLO

The son of Zeus and Leto, Apollo was born at Delos at the same time as his sister Artemis. He had innumerable adventures with both nymphs and mortal females. He was shepherd, warrior, and god of music and poetry on Mount Parnassus, where he presided over the Muses; a healer-god and prophet, he was also the god of harmony and of the moral virtues. Apollo became the deity of the Orphic cult, which promised salvation and eternal life to its initiates.

DEMETER-CORĒ

Demeter, goddess of nature and of the earth, was the daughter of Cronus and Rhea. Both in legend and in worship she was closely associated with her daughter Corē. The Eleusinian mysteries represented the episodes of the legend of the goddesses and revealed their profound meaning. For half the year Corē lived in the underworld with Hades, and during this time her mother's grief made the earth

barren. Corē returned to earth for the spring and summer. The cult of the goddesses, a remnant of the 'chthonian' or underworld religions, spread throughout Greece.

DIONYSUS

In the Classical period Dionysus was the god of the vine, of wine and of mystical delirium. His legend was complex, combining elements borrowed from Greece and the East. The son of Zeus and Semele, he was born from his father's thigh and entrusted to the care of Hermes. To save him from the jealousy of Hera, Zeus had to change him into a goat and hide him in Asia Minor. Dionysus travelled afar, discovering the vine and visiting Hades. The god of joy and frenzy, he ruled over the Satyrs, the Maenades and the Bacchantes and was honoured by wild processions followed by dramatic performances. Also the god of hope in a future life, he became in the Hellenistic period the protector of the secret sects which worshipped him by the celebration of the 'mysteries'.

PALLAS ATHENA

The daughter of Zeus and Metis, Athena emerged fully armed from the head of her father. A warrior goddess, she intervened in combats and gave assistance to Achilles, Ulysses and Hercules. The protection accorded to these heroes symbolized the aid which the spirit brings to brute strength and personal merit. Athena was regarded, especially in her own city, Athens, as the goddess of reason and presided over the arts and literature. Her beneficent intervention was extended to peace: she gave Athens the olive tree and protected craftsmen. Numerous cities adopted her as their protectress. Athena remained a virgin. Her attributes were the spear and the helmet, her emblem the owl.

POSEIDON

Poseidon, the son of Cronus and Rhea, and the brother of Zeus, was the god of the waters – sea, rivers, lakes and springs – and of storms. Athena took Athens from him, but he possessed his own island, Atlantis. His wife was Amphitrite, but he had countless liaisons, many of which resulted in the birth of malevolent Giants. Poseidon is to be found at the origin of many mythical genealogies; by Demeter he had a daughter whose name it was forbidden to utter. He was represented on a chariot, armed with a trident, surrounded with fishes and all kinds of marine creatures.

ZEUS

Having been saved from the cruelty of Cronus by his mother's cunning, Zeus was reared in Crete and returned to Olympus to dethrone his father. He established his dominion over the world, ruling on Olympus with his children, brothers and sisters among whom he divided his powers, while remaining the master of both men and gods. His spouse was Hera, but he entered into union with numer-

Cycladic idol (20th century BC)
Cretan goddess (12th century BC)
Archaic idol (7th century BC)
Pebble mosaics at Pella (4th century BC)
Lion hunt
Dionysus and the panther

ous goddesses and mortal women, begetting gods and heroes who appear in various legends. The god of light, of the sky and of the thunderbolt, and the guardian of the social hierarchy, he maintained order and authority in the world. This conception of Zeus as a universal power developed from the Homeric poems and was accepted throughout the Greek world. In the Hellenistic period Zeus was regarded by the Stoics as the symbol of the one and only god.

THE HEROES

Usually the offspring of a human being and a divinity, the heroes belonged to an intermediate order between the divine and the human. They received assistance from the gods, were endowed with superhuman strength and accomplished extraordinary exploits. Achilles, Perseus, Theseus and Hercules were all mortal, and yet the most famous of them, Hercules, was admitted to Olympus. Heroes could also be ordinary mortals to whom the gods had granted a special destiny (Oedipus, Orestes). The Greeks honoured the heroes with special cults, regarding them as intermediaries between gods and humans.

ACHILLES

Son of a mortal, Peleus, and the goddess Thetis, Achilles was raised by the Centaur Chiron. Bathed in the Styx by his mother, his body was invulnerable except for the heel by which she held him. He preferred a short but glorious life to a long and obscure existence. At the siege of Troy he was the bravest of the Greeks; to avenge the death of his friend Patroclus, Achilles killed Hector and dragged his corpse round the city. Legends of later date than the *Iliad* relate that he was himself killed by an arrow in the heel fired by Paris, the least courageous of the Trojans. The memory of Achilles, the hero of warrior strength and valour, remained very much alive in the popular imagination and his cult was widespread.

HERCULES

Son of Zeus and Alcmene, Hercules was pursued by the jealous Hera and had to submit to his cousin Eurystheus, who imposed on him twelve terrible ordeals. Hercules accomplished the twelve 'labours' not only by physical strength, but by his tenacity and moral courage. He came to a tragic end: after killing his children in a fit of madness, he committed suicide by having himself burnt on a pyre – but he was taken up to Olympus to dwell among the gods. The hero of Argos, Hercules was honoured by the Greeks as the embodiment of physical and moral strength overcoming all the evils which threaten humanity.

OEDIPUS

Laius, king of Thebes, who had learned from an oracle that his son would kill him and marry his mother, abandoned Oedipus at birth. Oedipus was reared by the king of Corinth, believing himself to be his son. When he heard of the oracle he fled to prevent its prediction from being fulfilled. In the course of his journey he killed an old man; then he succeeded in solving the riddle of the Sphinx and thereby rid Thebes of the monster. In gratitude the city offered him its kingship and the hand of Jocasta, the king's widow. When Oedipus discovered that he had unwittingly killed his father and married his mother, he blinded himself and fled with his daughter Antigone to Athens, where he died. In seeking to thwart the oracle's prediction, he had contributed to its fulfilment. The myth of a divinely ordained tragic fatality, against which man is powerless, was one of the most popular in Greece.

ORESTES

When Orestes was only a child, his mother Clytemnestra murdered his father Agamemnon, the King of Kings of the Trojan War, with the help of her lover Aegisthus. Orestes fled, but returned a few years later, with his friend Pylades, and avenged his father by killing Clytemnestra and Aegisthus. This act of parricide provoked the wrath of the gods and the Erinyes, the maleficent deities of vengeance, pursued him everywhere. Apollo took pity on Orestes, who had only done his filial duty, and pleaded on his behalf before an Athenian tribunal, the Areopagus. Orestes was acquitted and purged of his defilement at Delphi. The merciful intervention of Apollo had lifted the ancient curse which Zeus had laid on the family of the Atridae.

THESEUS

Theseus was the hero of Attica and the counterpart of Hercules, the Dorian hero. He was supposed to have lived a generation before the Trojan War. In his youth he accomplished a series of tasks similar to those of Hercules in the Peloponnesus. Later he killed the Minotaur in Crete, thus liberating Attica from a bloody tribute. On his return he founded Athens by bringing twelve townships together. He also distinguished himself in the war against the Amazons. Theseus is the archetype of the adventurer-hero and was honoured by Athens as its founder and liberator.

ULYSSES

Much more than Achilles, Ulysses is the ideal Greek hero. He was one of the architects of the Greek victory over the Trojans, but above all he is the hero of the *Odyssey* in which Homer recounts the adventures of his return to Ithaca, where Penelope awaited him. Ulysses is profoundly human, his companions are his friends as well as his subjects. Full of valour, he never retreated from danger, but he relied on his wits rather than on courage and strength: it was in this way that he triumphed over the Cyclops, the Sirens and the sorceress Circé. A victim of the divine rivalries of Poseidon and Athena, he personified the Hellenic ideal of the man of reason and moderation, endowed with a fiery energy.

Greek Art in the Archaic, Classical and Hellenistic Periods

After the glorious achievements of the Cretan and Mycenaean cultures, the Dorian invasions of the twelfth century BC marked the beginning of a dark age not only for the arts of Greece, but for her entire civilization. Several centuries later art reappeared, but with hardly any trace of the Cretan and Mycenaean traditions. This birth of Greek art proper can be observed in pottery: about 900 BC the *proto-Geometric* style of the tenth century was succeeded by the *Geometric* style in which the ornamentation of vases combined geometrical motifs with stylized figures of persons and animals. Between 850 and 750 the first temples were built, though distinctly primitive in their architecture. The re-emergence of sculpture was equally modest, the little bronzes of the eighth century showing a close resemblance to the human figures on pottery.

Although immensely appealing, Geometric art remained rudimentary. The decisive step forward was to be taken in the Archaic period (750–550), culminating within less than three centuries in the full flowering of the Classical age. This progress was due to the stabilization of society and to contacts with the East.

ARCHITECTURE

RELIGIOUS BUILDINGS

Greek monumental architecture was almost solely religious until the Hellenistic period. The temple was the dwelling of the god and housed his statue, but religious life – processions and sacrifices – took place outside the temple. The classic plan of the temple comprised three parts: the *pronaos*, an entrance porch; the *naos* or sanctuary proper; and the *opisthodomos*, a porch behind the *naos* and symmetrical with the *pronaos*. Depending on the function of the temple, its plan could be more complex: the secret cults required an *adyton* or 'holy of holies' at the end of the *naos* (the Temple of Apollo at Delphi, for example). At the Parthenon two rooms were built behind the *naos* to hold the treasure of Athens. Columns stood along one, two or four sides of the edifice.

Architecture comprised three 'orders' distinguished mainly by the style of the column. The *Doric order*, which originated in the Peloponnesus, is characterized by a sturdy column without a base.

Its capital has a circular echinus and a square abacus. The architrave is smooth and the frieze formed by the alternation of triglyphs (panels decorated with vertical grooves) and metopes (square panels, usually carved). The *Ionic order* originated in the Hellenized regions of Asia and in the islands. Its column, much more slender, rests on a base. The capital is adorned with volutes. The architrave is composed of three bands one above the other. The frieze, when there is one, forms a perfect ground for a continuous series of sculptures. The decorative profusion of the continuous frieze marks an Eastern influence. These two orders, at first quite opposite in conception, are usually found combined in the same building in the Classical period (the Doric order on the outside, the Ionic inside). The *Corinthian order* is merely a variation on the Ionic order, from which it is distinguished by its capital with volutes concealed under acanthus leaves. It appeared at the end of the fifth century BC (temple of Bassae-Phigalia), developing in the fourth century and in the Hellenistic period.

CIVIL BUILDINGS

The stone theatre appeared in the fourth century BC. It comprised three parts: the tiers or *koilon*, in a semi-circle round the orchestra, were divided by a circular promenade (*diazoma*); in the centre of the *orchestra* stood an altar dedicated to Dionysus (it was here that the choruses performed). The *skēnē*, a rectangular structure, served as wings. The columns of the *proskenion* supported the scenery; the actors performed in front of it, on a stage above the orchestra.

There were various buildings reserved for sport, including the *stadion*, the *gymnasion* and the *palaistra* for the training of athletes. Meetings were also held on the *agora*, a public square bordered by colonnades (*stoa*), especially in the Hellenistic period.

SCULPTURE

From the eighth century BC man was the major theme of sculpture. The *kouros* ('youth') and the *korē* ('maiden'), bearers of offerings, appeared in the late seventh century. The *kouros* is a naked youth, standing with his arms by his sides and with

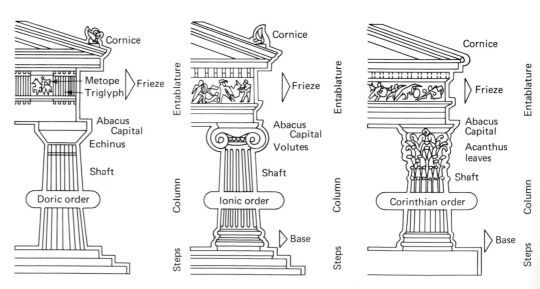

his left leg slightly forward. The *korē,* draped in a tunic and a mantle, holds an offering in her right hand. Only the rendering of the bodies varied from one school to another. At the same time, the Greeks devised the rules governing the decoration of the upper parts of the temple, the frieze and the pediment. From the end of the sixth century, the representation of the human body and face became increasingly lifelike.

A similar severity influenced the sculpture of the early Classical age. The two finest works discovered are bronzes: the *Poseidon* from Cape Artemision and the *Charioteer* from Delphi. The monumental sculpture of this period is represented by the decoration of the Temple of Zeus at Olympia. In the following generation, Phidias executed the gold and ivory statues of Zeus and Athena Parthenos, and also the decoration of the Parthenon, while Myron (the *Discobulus*) and Polycletus (the *Doryphorus* and *Diadumenus*) carved athletes. In the fourth century

the search for refinement and grace continued, and faces became more expressive of the inner life. Praxiteles carved graceful, languid bodies (*Hermes, Aphrodite of Cnidus*). Scopas conveyed human anxiety, producing countless specially commissioned statues and collaborating on the mausoleum at Halicarnassus. Lysippus continued the studies which Polycletus had made of the human body (*Apoxyomenos*) and became Alexander's sculptor. Hellenistic sculpture enjoyed an extraordinary flowering in the schools of Alexandria, Syria, Delos and Rhodes (Chares of Lindos carved the *Colossus of Rhodes* in the early third century BC, while the *Laöcoon* dates from the first century BC); at the same time, in Greece itself inspiration seemed to be running dry. The Roman conquest was to lead to the widespread diffusion of sculpture in Italy and its adaptation to more cold and conventional forms.

PAINTING AND POTTERY

In the almost total absence of original works, the only evidence of Greek painting is to be found in literary references or in the copies made in pottery and mosaic from the fourth century onwards. A few names are known: Polygnotus of Thasos, the painter of the *Leschē of the Cnidians* at Delphi (early fifth century), and his rival Mikon, Zeuxis (late fifth) and Apelles (fourth century), official sculptor to Alexander the Great.

The evolution of pottery is easier to trace. In the Archaic period, the influence of the East made figures more supple and introduced new themes; the *Oriental style* developed chiefly at Rhodes and Corinth, which exported its vases throughout the Mediterranean. In the sixth century a new technique emerged, the *black figure.* Henceforth, man was represented more often than animals or

flowers. The workshops of Athens were the most active and famous. One of their artists, Exekias, painted mythological scenes in minute detail during the second half of the sixth century. Towards 530 BC the *red figure* appeared, with the background of the vessel entirely black and the decoration in the natural colour of the clay. The art of silhouette gradually made way for genuine painting and an art of much greater subtlety.

The Painter of Andokides, Euthymides, the Painter of Kleophrades, and the Painter of Brygos and Douris were the leading exponents of the *severe style* (530–480). This was followed by the *free style* (480–380); the Painter of Penthesilea, the Painter of the Niobides and Polygnotus painted figures whose strongly marked gestures expressed violent feelings. This style foreshadowed Hellenistic art. The *flowery style* (the Painter of Meidias) is characterized by its mannered elegance. In the fourth century, Athenian production continued (*Kertsch style*), but the pottery was much less carefully finished.

In the Hellenistic period, pottery declined, though it did not disappear; the human figure was abandoned in favour of plant motifs.

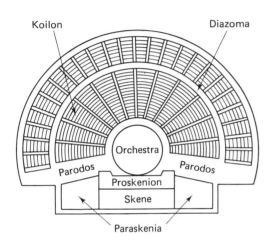

Tourist Itineraries and Suggestions

This book is divided into four distinct parts so that the visitor can arrange an itinerary based on one or more sections according to the time at his or her disposal.

1. ATHENS
(3–4 days)

Theseus is supposed to have assembled several villages of Attica to form the city of Athens, which is why its name is in the plural (*Athenai* in Greek). One should spend at least three days there. Here is a suggested programme:

1st day
Morning:
Acropolis, Acropolis Museum and Areopagus (2 hrs).
Afternoon:
The ancient part of the city, the monument of Lysicratus, the Tower of the Winds, the library of Hadrian, the Byzantine churches of the Kapnikarea and the Little Metropolis, the Agora, the Hephaisteion (Theseion), the Pnyx, the Hill of the Muses and the monument of Philopappus, where there is a beautiful view of Athens at sunset (3 hrs).

2nd day
Morning:
National Museum (2 hrs).
Afternoon:
Excursion to the monastery of Kaisariani [7 km from Athens] and Cape Sounion [70 km] (4 hrs).

3rd day
Morning:
Byzantine Museum (1–2 hrs), Benaki Museum with its wonderful Oriental collections (1 hr).
Afternoon:
Excursion to Eleusis (see the beginning of Chapter 2) and the monastery of Daphni (2½ hrs).
A fourth day will be necessary if you want to be able to make a second visit to the National Museum and spend a little time strolling through the city. The Plaka district has lost much of its charm, but here one can still enjoy the provincial life of this great city, with its newspaper kiosks, shoeblacks, and vendors of lottery-tickets and sponges. The National Garden in the city-centre is a delightful spot for a walk. Constitution Square (Plateia Syntagmatos) offers a little oasis of greenery that often passes unnoticed; there are cool, shaded cafés bordering the lawn.

The recently built museum of modern painting (opposite the Hilton hotel) contains some interesting pictures bequeathed by Greek collectors (including works by El Greco).

Life comes to a halt throughout Greece from 2.30 to 5 p.m., the time of the siesta.

It is difficult to recommend a restaurant in Athens (see 'Food and Drink', p. 169). Most visitors dine in Plaka, the Montmartre of Athens, or in the fish restaurants at Tourkolimano (the yacht harbour at Piraeus, 10 km from Athens), or at Glyphada (16 km) with its fashionable Astir beach. At Glyphada the Psaropoulos restaurant offers simplicity and quality. Hotels are numerous in Athens and of all categories (AAA, AA, A, B, C). The most luxurious are the Hilton (with swimming-pool) and the Grande Bretagne (AAA). Also to be recommended are the Amalia (AA), the Electra (A), the Royal Olympic (A), the Lykabette (B) and, at Vouliagmani by the sea, the very luxurious and pleasant Astir Palace (AAA), 20 km from Athens.

2. DELPHI AND THE PELOPONNESUS
(5 days)

This second chapter is devoted to the main archaeological sites of Greece. The excursion, which takes five to six days, can be made either by private car or by coach (the C.H.A.T. organization is excellent and offers a wide variety of tours). One can also visit Delphi and the Peloponnesus in two separate excursions; in this case, two days should be allowed for Delphi (with a visit to the monastery of Hosios Levkas) and four days for the Peloponnesus. A motorway links Athens with Corinth and Patras, passing through some magnificent countryside. To reach the Peloponnesus direct from Delphi you can either take a ferry at Itea for Aigion (3 hrs crossing), or continue along the road beyond Delphi through the valleys of the Parnassus mountains as far as Nafpaktos and Antirion, where a ferry will take you to Rion (45 mins). The scenery is superb. Plenty of hotels at Delphi (the Amalia is particularly pleasant) and at Olympia (S.P.A.P., Xenia). The Xenia hotels have been built by the Greek government (there is one at Sparta and another at Nauplia). In Nauplia the Amphytrion hotel is also worth mentioning. One can have a good lunch at the Xenia hotel at Mycenae or at the Belle Hélène, and at the tourist pavilion in Corinth.

3. AEGINA, THE METEORA, RHODES AND CRETE
(9–12 days)

This section offers various excursions starting from Athens:

● The boat-trip to Aegina from Piraeus can be made in a day. As the boats also serve Poros, Hydra and Spetsai, a combined visit to these islands can easily be made in three or four days.

● The excursion to the Meteora takes two or three days, by car or coach (C.H.A.T.), stopping at Volos (museum with Hellenistic painted stelae from Demetrios), a town that was badly damaged by an earthquake in 1955. Stay the night at Kalambaka (Divani and Xenia hotels). From Volos you can also take the opportunity to explore the beautiful countryside of Mount Pelion, walking through its forests which run down to the sea and enjoying the charm of its old dwellings. In this case you should allow an extra day or two and stay at Portaria or Tsangarada.

● A visit to Rhodes and Crete, if not made during a sea-cruise, can be included in a tour by aeroplane from Athens lasting four to five days. There are several flights daily. Rhodes is an excellently equipped tourist resort with over fifty hotels, the most luxurious being the Grand Hotel (AAA), the Hotel des Roses (AA, the oldest) and the Metropolitan Kapsis (the most recent). The Miramar Beach and

make sure that the person in charge of the boat knows enough English for you to make your intentions clear, in order to avoid unpleasant misunderstandings. Read carefully the contract which you are given listing the conditions of hire – your own food is an extra (the crew's food and the fuel are usually included in the cost of hire) – and arrange an itinerary before signing the contract.

● Apart from the big international cruises, a number of Greek shipping firms organize cruises in Greek waters. Especially recommended are the cruises of the Sun Line on the *Stella Maris* and the *Stella Oceanis* (seven days, departing from Piraeus on Mondays): Heraklion, Santorin, Rhodes, Ephesus, Istanbul, Delos and Mykonos.

● Many islands now have their own comfortable hotels. Corfu offers a variety of choice, from the luxurious Corfu Palace and Miramare Beach (bungalows) to the Club Méditerranée and, in between, some delightful small hotels such as the Pension Suisse. Other recommended hotels on the islands are: Chios (Xenia, B), Hydra (Hydra Beach, A; Miramare, A; Xenia, B), Tinos (Beach Hotel, A), Lemnos (Akti-Myrina bungalow-hotel), Mykonos (Leto, A; Afroditi, B; Xenia, B), Paros (Naoussa, B; Xenia, B), Paxos (Paxos Beach, bungalows), a charming little Ionian island with its twin island of Anti-Paxos, Poros (Motel, B), Santorin (Atlantis, B), Skiathos (Hesperides, A; Xenia, B), Skopelos (Xenia, B), Spetsai (Xenia, B) and Thasos (Makryamnos).
One can also rent houses (but make sure you see them first to avoid disappointment) or rooms from the local inhabitants, which is often a very pleasant way of entering into the simplicity of Greek life.

the Golden Beach are hotels with individual bungalows (A). You should allow half a day for visiting the medieval town (Collachium, the Palace of the Grand Masters, the museum and the fortifications) and at least another half-day for Lindos (55 km from Rhodes). But you should also give yourself time for a bathe and for walking along the little roads of the island (Petaloudes, the 'valley of butterflies', is 25 km from the town).

● For those who like adventure and discovery there is the Maina region in the southern Peloponnesus. Fierce mountain-dwellers and redoubtable warriors, the Mainotes lived in tower-houses rather like those of Tuscany in the thirteenth century; they came to Rome as soldiers and founded the village of Carghese in Corsica, and they still have one tradition in common with the Corsicans: the vendetta. The whole of the southern Peloponnesus is an ideal region for walking.

● Without giving away too many secrets, the author suggests the following islands as offering special qualities of their own: Kythira, Siphnos, Naxos, Santorin, Skopelos and Paxos.

● Crete also requires at least two days: Knossos (3 hrs), the museum (2 hrs), and the excursion to Phaestus and Haghia Triada 60 km from Heraklion (4 hrs). You might find Alexandros, who achieved fame in Henry Miller's *The Colossus of Maroussi*, still watching over the ruins of Phaestus. For a long time the hotels at Heraklion were of mediocre quality. However, the Astir, the Astoria and the new bungalow-hotels on the neighbouring beaches (Creta Beach, Cnossos Beach) can be recommended. But Crete offers a much more exciting adventure, and if you are not too concerned about comfort you could spend your entire holiday discovering this wild and wonderful island. For those who prefer a fixed base there are some marvellous beaches and good hotels at Haghios Nikolaos, Minos Beach, Elounda Beach and Mirambello.

4. THE ISLANDS

● For hiring yachts, caiques, etc., ask for the list of approved agents at the Greek Tourist Office. But

● Anyone fond of Byzantine art should go to Salonica (Thessaloniki; numerous flights daily from Athens), the second most important city of Greece, where there are some beautiful churches: Haghios Georgios (fifth century), Haghia Sophia (eighth century, mosaics of the tenth century), the Panaghia Chalkeon (eleventh century) and the basilica of Haghios Dimitrios which, though recently rebuilt after a fire, still has some fascinating frescoes and mosaics. The churches in the upper town should also be seen: Haghia Ekaterini (thirteenth century), Hosios David with its rare fifth-century mosaic; and, of course, the archaeological museum. The ancient Macedonian capital, Pella, lies only 40 km from Thessaloniki and its little museum possesses some beautiful Hellenistic pebble-mosaics (Dionysus on a panther and the lion hunt reproduced on p. 163).

● There are also many small museums with interesting collections: Corinth, Thebes, Nauplia, Argos, Nemea, Sparta, Volos, Corfu, Mykonos, Samos and Lesbos (the Theopelos museum).

General Information and Advice

READING

● As a general introduction to Greek civilization the book by the great English classical scholar, C M Bowra, *The Greek Experience*, is easy to read.

A Concise History of Ancient Greece by Peter Green (available only in Great Britain) deals with every aspect of Greek Antiquity and is copiously illustrated, and *Ancient Greece: An Illustrated History* (available in the USA) is also an interesting and authoritative book.

The outstanding study of Greek mythology is unquestionably *Greek Myths* by Robert Graves.

The *History of the Peloponnesian War* by Thucydides is hard reading but fascinating nonetheless. The *Description of Greece* by Pausanias, a lively account of the author's travels written when ancient Greece was in decline, exists in a translation with commentary by J G Frazer (1898) and also in the Loeb Classical Library series.

A Handbook of Greek Art by G M A Richter offers a comprehensive study of the arts of ancient Greece with numerous illustrations.

The heights of Greek literature are accessible in translation; C M Bowra's *Ancient Greek Literature* provides a general study of Greek authors. *Greek Literature in Translation* by Michael Grant offers an excellent anthology of ancient Greek poetry and prose. Two works by F L Lucas, available in Great Britain under the titles *Greek Poetry for Everyman* and *Greek Drama for Everyman*, and in the USA under the titles *Greek Poetry* and *Greek Tragedy and Comedy*, present a wide selection of translated excerpts from the Greek poets and playwrights.

The Colossus of Maroussi is Henry Miller's hymn in praise of Greece. Lawrence Durrell's *Reflections on a Marine Venus* is an evocative account of the island of Rhodes and *Prospero's Cell* about Corfu. A very useful and authoritative book which gives much more detailed information on the history and mythology of ancient Greece is *Classics Illustrated Dictionary* by J W Fuchs.

The most popular modern Greek novels are those of Nikos Kazantzakis (*Zorba the Greek, Christ Recrucified, The Last Temptation of Christ*). Greece has some fine modern poets little known outside their own country (Kavafy, Palamas, Seferis, Sikerianos).

SEASONS, FESTIVALS AND TRADITIONS

● The spring is not the best season for visiting Greece. It can be cold and wet in April and the sea is rarely warm enough before the beginning of June. In July and August it is very hot and the country is overcrowded with tourists. September and October are delicious months in Greece, and the weather can often remain fine up to Christmas.

● Festivals in Greece are occasions of great importance and splendour, for the Greeks have preserved strong religious traditions; the principal saints are Basil (Vassilis), Nicholas (patron-saint of sailors) and George (a legendary saint, prince of Cappadocia, martyred under Diocletian).

The first day of the year is the feast of Haghios Vassilis. In Greece the Epiphany takes priority over Christmas; on the islands, after the celebration of the liturgy, the priest throws his cross into the waters of the harbour and the local boys fight to recover it. 25 March is both the feast of the Virgin (the Annunciation) and a national holiday (Declaration of Independence). The Kathara Theftera is a day of rejoicing before the beginning of Lent (the youngsters take part in kite-flying competitions). Easter, the great popular and religious festival of the year, is celebrated with much gaiety. The people eat lamb roasted on a spit in the open air. On 15 August the Assumption is celebrated, the great summer festival; there are numerous processions, the most famous of which is that of Tinos, a 'miraculous' place of pilgrimage renowned throughout Greece. 28 October is another national day, commemorating the heroic Greek resistance to the Italian declaration of war.

● Singing, dancing and music in Greece have preserved some lively traditions. The *bouzouki* (mandoline) is at the origin of a whole musical style, the *bouzoukia*, brought from Asia by the Greek refugees and made fashionable after the Second World War by gifted musicians such as Hadjidakis and Theodorakis.

The *kalamatianos* or *syrtos* is a joyous peasant dance in 7/8 time popular all over Greece. The *zebetiko* is a mysterious solo dance originally connected with a secret sect and has a strange 9/8 rhythm; it is sometimes performed in tavernas by a customer who has been suddenly inspired. The *hassapiko* is a gay dance performed by two or three young people, whose movements are identical; it was danced by Alexis Zorba (in the film it was wrongly called *sirtaki*). The *tsamiko* is a heroic dance which came from Epirus and is popular throughout the Peloponnesus; only one of the two men actually dances, the other guiding his partner with a handkerchief. The Greeks love songs and in the night-clubs of Athens one can hear the latest stars performing.

THE GREEKS

The Greek race for a long time seemed physically unattractive, doubtless because of lack of nourishment. Beauty was found in the men – the *pallikaria* or 'valiant young men' – and rarely in the women. The admixture of Albanian blood in the sixteenth and seventeenth centuries appears to have played an important role; towards the middle of the nineteenth century the descendants of this sturdy mountain people seem to have formed twenty per cent of the Greek population. Another decisive contribution was that made by the Greeks of Asia Minor in 1923 (over one million out of the total population of six millions); the heirs of Byzantium, many of them having occupied important positions under the Ottoman domination, they played their part in the intellectual and physical regeneration of Greece. Today the Greeks appear to be blossoming, and among young men and women one finds the dazzling beauty of ancient times returning.

This race, the product of innumerable inter-mixtures, is courageous, intelligent, active and sober. It possesses a great curiosity of mind and an acute sense of individuality. In spite of political upheavals it has always displayed a passionate love of its country (the fabulously wealthy Koundoriatis ruined himself for the liberation of Greece, and a patron of the arts like Benaki presented his priceless collections to his fellow-countrymen). In Greece there is a generosity of heart which, though it might sometimes seem a little rash, creates the nobility of this people. Many Greeks treat all mankind as their friends and this open-heartedness works miracles, bringing out the best in everyone.

In Athens everybody is selling something – sponges, lottery-tickets, nuts, dolls – and even a meal in a tavern will be interrupted by discreet approaches from a pedlar. Do not be surprised to see Greeks frequently fingering large beads (*komboi*); this habit has no particular religious significance, but is simply a way of relaxing (much more graceful than chewing gum).

FOOD AND DRINK

Katsymbalis, the hero of *The Colossus of Maroussi*, told me that there were only two kinds of food in the world, French and Greek, a judgement highly flattering to Greek cuisine. About ten years ago one could enjoy tasty meals in Greece; is it the fault of tourism that Greek food nowadays seems so insipid? My Greek friends have themselves admitted that they are unable to recommend a single good restaurant in Athens.

With fish – perch, sea-bream and red mullet sprinkled with oil – you are not likely to be too disappointed. Greek *hors-d'oeuvre* are excellent: *dolmadakia* or *dolmades* (vine-leaves with rice), *taramosalata* (fish roes, bread, oil and onion), *melitzanosalata* (crushed aubergine, oil and onion), *sadjiki* (yoghurt, cucumber and oil). There is also the Turkish heritage: tas khebab, beurrek (*tiropatadika*, a pie of strong cheese), *moussaka* (minced aubergine, meat and onion). Greece has a vegetable of its own, the *bamias*, green and tender, shaped like tiny gherkins. The goat's cheese, *feta*, is dry and scented. Young lamb is a dish for special occasions; spiny lobster (langouste) is easily obtainable on most islands.

As for wine, the Greek *retsina* (white wine mixed with resin) is an acquired taste and, to be palatable, the resin flavour should not be too strong. The white wines of Achaia are pleasant (Haghia Helena), as are the red wines of Thessaly (Buttaris). The wine of Rhodes (Chevalier) is more fruity and has a higher alcoholic content. The Greeks drink a lot of water and can talk at great length about its flavour. Pindar remarked that water and gold were the best things in the world.

Turkish coffee is served on request and under a variety of names, depending on its strength and sugar-content. Westerners usually prefer it *metrio* (medium); it can also be *variglikos* (strong and very sweet), *sketos* (without sugar), *glikivrastos* (sweet, without grounds), *elafrisglikos* (slightly sugared) and so on.

SHOPPING AND GIFTS

There is little that a spoilt Westerner is tempted to buy in Greece. If some Greek friends accompany you to the airport you will leave the country with pistachio nuts (which are exquisite) and a bottle of *ouzo*, the national aniseed drink.

ATHENS

Gold jewellery copied from ancient models is obtainable at *Zolotas*, which has branches in London, New York and Paris, and at *Ilias Lalaounis*; handwoven articles at *Anna Sikelianou*, 1 Panou; rugs and embroideries at *Vassiliki*, Pronia. Also: *To mati*, 20 Vankourestiou, and. *Lykion Ellinedon* (Greek costumes); the street of the antique shops (Pandrossou) borders the Plaka district (*Martinos* has the rarest antiques); another antique shop to be recommended is *Antiqua*, 4 Amalia. For those fond of old books about Greece and engravings there are bookshops at 9 Valaoritou and 6 Solonos.

MYKONOS

Maroulina's jewellery shop is known all over the world. Vassilios Nikou makes model boats.

AEGINA

Paintings of seascapes by Petros Kaltzes (the Pelagisios).

SKYROS

Famous for its handicrafts (pottery, embroidery, carved wood), unfortunately in decline.

CONVERSATION

The Greek language takes a long time to learn, but one soon picks up the few essential words: *kalimera, kalispera, kalinikta* (good morning, good evening, good night); *effkaristo poli* (thank you very much); *krassi* (wine); *barbouni* (mullet), *sinagrida* (sea-bass); *yasou!* (to your health! hallo!); and one vital expression, *po-po-po-po*, the equivalent of the French *Oh! là là!* The shop signs provide an opportunity to familiarize yourself with the Greek alphabet.

A.B.

169

Contents

This volume, the third in the 'Observed' series, was written and produced by André Barret.

The supplementary information was written by Anne-Marie Sorbets.

Most of the Greek texts cited are taken from 'Anthologie de la Poésie grecque' by Robert Brasillach (Ed. Stock).

The following photographers collaborated on the illustrations in this book, Messrs: Scouroyannis – Kondos – Hassia – Reichel – Boubat – Hannibal – Séraf – Meletzis – Loirat – Francastel – Lessing, Manos, Riboud, Morath, Burri, Cartier-Bresson (Magnum) – Trutmann – Roiter – Stournaras – Viollon, Boisnard (Rapho) – de Sazo, Garanger, Hirmer, Simon, Darr, Charbonnier, Millet (Réalités) – Klein, Frieman, Lacarrière, Lebel, Lénars. Agence Giraudon and Agence Girardet.

Already published in this series:
Moscow and Leningrad Observed
Spain Observed   *France Observed*
Florence Observed   *Paris Observed*
Israel Observed   *Egypt Observed*

First published in Great Britain by
Kaye & Ward Ltd
21 New Street, London EC2M 4NT
1974   Reprinted 1979

First published in the USA by
Oxford University Press Inc.
200 Madison Avenue, New York, NY 10016
1974   Reprinted 1979

ISBN 0 7182 1002 6 (Great Britain)
ISBN 0 19 519779 8 (USA)
Library of Congress Catalog Card Number 74-75764

Printed in Italy
by Officine Grafiche Arnoldo Mondadori, Verona